Rav Zvi Dov Kanotopsky

THE DEPTHS OF SIMPLICITY

Incisive Essays on the Torah

בראשית
שמות
ויקרא

Genesis Jerusalem Press
5754/1994

© Copyright 1994
Originally published as *Night of Watching*.

All rights reserved. No part of this publication may be translated, reproduced, stored in a retrieval system or transmitted, **in any form** or by any means, electronic, mechanical, photocopying, recording or otherwise, without prior permission in writing from the publisher. Printed in Israel. The rights of the copyright holder will be strictly enforced.

Typeset by: *Dagush International*
Ma'ale Amos,
D.N. Jerusalem Hills
Israel 90966

ISBN 0-9630936-3-0

10 9 8 7 6 5 4 3 2 1

Distributed by:
Feldheim Publishers Ltd.
POB 35002 / Jerusalem, Israel

Philipp Feldheim Inc.
200 Airport Executive Park
Spring Valley, NY 10977

Printed in Israel

THE DEPTHS OF SIMPLICITY

This book is dedicated to the memory of

Dr. Steven F. Stein ע"ה

שמעון פייביש בן יצחק הכהן

שלשה כתרים הן כתר תורה וכתר כהונה וכתר מלכות
וכתר שם טוב עולה על גביהן

by his wife and children

Mrs. Marilyn Stein Mantz

| David & Lisa Stein | Tami Stein |
| Cheryl & Avi Savitsky | Jonathan Stein |

ת.נ.צ.ב.ה.

and to our grandfather, father, & husband

Sam Gottleib ע"ה

שמואל אלכסנדר בן אליעזר ליפע

מסר את נפשו בעד עמו ובעד משפחתו

Mrs. Rose Gottleib

Elaine & Billy Millen	Marilyn & Harvey Mantz
Yehuda & Sharon Millen	David & Lisa Stein
Pia & Moshe Gross	Cheryl & Avi Savitsky
Penina & Jack Valenski	Tami Stein
Deena & Marvin Nagler	Jonathan Stein
Sharon Millen	

ת.נ.צ.ב.ה.

Contents

In Memoriam ix
Acknowledgments xi

Sefer Bereishith
  Parashath Bereishith
    The Seventh Day 15
  Parashath Noach
    Monument to Survival 20
  Parashath Lech Lecha
    The Lonely Way 25
  Parashath VaYeira
    Man's Struggle for Justice 29
  Parashath Chayei Sarah
    Sarah's Influence 34
  Parashath Toledoth
    Mother of Nations 39
  Parashath VaYeitzei
    Family Strength 44
  Parashath VaYishlach
    Chariot of God 49
  Parashath VaYeishev
    The Inheritance 55
  Parashath MiKeitz
    Brotherly Spies 60
  Parashath VaYigash
    Reconciliation 65
  Parashath VaYechi
    The Provider versus Royalty 69

Sefer Shemoth 75
  Parashath Shemoth
    The Leader's Trials 77
  Parashath VaEira
    The Naming 82

Parashath Bo
Night of Watching 87
Parashath Beshallach
Murmurings 91
Parashath Yithro
A Father's Role 95
Parashath Mishpatim
Human Freedom 99
Parashath Terumah
Holiness and Separation 103
Parashath Tetzaveh
Continuous Light 107
Parashath Ki Thissa
Seek the Miraculous 112
Parashath VaYakhel
Fire as a Symbol 117
Parashath Pekudei
Redeemed 121

Sefer VaYikra 125
Parashath VaYikra
The Offering 127
Parashath Tzav
The Burning Altar 131
Parashath Shemini
Bricks of Sapphire 136
Parashath Tazria
The Drama of Birth 141
Parashath Metzora
Slander 145
Parashath Acharei Moth
Laws and Statutes 149
Parashath Kedoshim
Be Holy 153
Parashath Emor
The Cycle of Festivals 157
Parashath BeHar
Commemorating Creation 161
Parashath BeChukkothai
The Uncircumcised Heart 165

In Memoriam

"OH HOW I LOVE YOUR TORAH! IT IS MY MEDITATION [CONVERSATION] ALL THE DAY." (Psalms 119:97)

This verse serves as the banner heralding the theme of the second book of Maimonides' *Mishneh Torah*. "The Book of Adoration" contains those *mizvoth* which, according to Maimonides' description, "are to be constantly observed and which we have been commanded to keep in order that we may always *love* God and be ever mindful of Him." The psalmist's love of and engrossment with Torah is applied by Maimonides to the all-embracing character of certain *mizvoth* and their call for regular and continuous involvement.

Yet, a simpler meaning of the verse — one which was reflected in the life of my father-in-law, zt"l — may be suggested. There are few people whose thoughts are constantly focused on Torah, whose probing and creative minds continuously seek a *chidush* in Torah, whose entire being is in a state of unrest in the absence of Torah study. Such a rare and precious person was Rav Kanotopsky, whose regular conversation always related to the elucidation of Torah texts and values.

"Oh how I love Your Torah! It is my meditation [conversation] all the day." The pages of this volume mirror a measure of Rav Kanotopsky's true love of Torah and represent only a portion of his regular meditations and conversations. Thus, the psalmist's love of Torah and daily involvement therewith may refer, in the case of rare individuals, not only to the totality of those *mizvoth* included in the Book of Adoration, but specifically to the sublime and exalted precept of Torah meditation and conversation.

May Rav Kanotopsky's love of Torah serve as a model to his students and to those privileged to know him. May his words of Torah reach and inspire those who seek both the simple and profound in Torah. May his memory be a blessing for Israel.

Menachem Meier

Acknowledgments

My husband, *zt"l*, author of this work, was a man of personal magnetism, stimulating imagination, and inspiring dedication to religious values. With Rabbi Dr. Joseph B. Soloveitchik as his mentor, he developed intellectually in the Brisker method and was a senior lecturer in Talmud, Jewish philosophy, and Bible at Yeshiva University for twenty-eight years. He also served as a congregational rabbi in Crown Heights, Brooklyn, and West Hempstead, Long Island.

After his *aliyah* in 1970, he headed Machon LeTalmud and was senior lecturer in Bible at both Hebrew University and Michlalah-Jerusalem College for Women. His passion was researching the classic commentaries on the Bible and Talmud.

I thank my dear children: Menachem and Zipora Meier, Judith and Yisroel Abramovitz, and Joseph and Shlomit Kanotopsky. Their encouragement allowed me to produce this work, and their reading the text and typing and correcting footnotes added a personal note of love to the love of Torah.

With heartfelt gratitude, I acknowledge the participation

of the following persons in preparing this volume: Rabbi Dr. Meier Fulda of Yeshiva University; Rabbi Dr. Zeev Gottlieb, *av beith din* of Glasgow; Prof. Chaim Levine of the Bar Ilan University Talmud dept.; Rabbi Dr. Menachem Meier of the Frisch School, New Jersey; Prof. Alice Shalvi of the Hebrew University, English-literature dept.; Rabbi Dr. Aryeh Strikofsky of Torah LaGolah; Rabbi Azreal Wolfson of Savyon, Israel; Dr. Aviva Zornberg; and Moshe Shalvi and Eli Stein, my printing advisors.

Sincerely,
Shoshana Kanotopsky, Editor
Jerusalem

ספר בראשית
Sefer Bereishith
The Book of Genesis

פרשת בראשית
Parashath Bereishith

The Seventh Day

ויברך אלקים את יום השביעי ויקדש אתו....
"GOD BLESSED THE SEVENTH DAY AND SANCTIFIED IT...."
(Genesis 2:3)

Many translations and interpretations of this *pasuk* have been suggested in our commentaries. Rashi[1] interprets the blessing and sanctification here as referring to manna, the heavenly food that the children of Israel enjoyed during their journey through the wilderness. According to Rashi, "blessed — *vayevarech*" implies that God provided a double portion of the manna on the sixth day of Creation; "sanctified — *vaykadesh*" means that no manna fell on the seventh day.

Rashi's interpretation gives rise to some very significant ideas that are relevant to this context and in keeping with the unfolding drama of Creation.

The Torah indicates that heaven, earth, and their hosts were completed by the end of the first six days. Ramban[2] notes that the heavens and the earth have hosts. The heavens' consists of the celestial bodies and all the physical phenomena above the earth, while the earth's consists of the earth itself, its elements, and its resources. The statement that the hosts were completed[3] implies that they were ready to function together for the express purpose of producing the vegetation necessary to sustain life. At this point, the Torah introduces the concept of the sanctity of the seventh day, Shabbath, and the metanatural reaction that occurs only through the will of God. In fact, vegetation is also possible through the will of God even in the absence of any physical or natural agency. The manna in the wilderness — a food supplied by God directly from heaven, with no apparent reliance upon the "hosts" of the heavens or the earth — therefore impresses upon us a basic religious truth: The food that does derive from the very real physical interaction of nature's elements is provided by a higher power and represents the will and kindness of God.

Rashi's interpretation captures the essence of the religious message of this seventh day. It is a source of blessing and sanctification. The basic theme of Shabbath is that bread does not depend upon these "hosts."

We can regard our theme from yet another perspective: In the Ten Commandments in Exodus, the Torah predicates the observance of Shabbath on the theme of Creation.[4] In Deuteronomy, however, the observance of Shabbath is related to the drama of the exodus from Egypt.[5] Rambam maintains in *Guide for the Perplexed*[6] that there are indeed two motivations behind the observance of Shabbath. First, it impresses upon us the truth of Creation. Second, it impresses upon us the freedom we attained through the exodus, thus making it possible for us to rest as free men.

In his commentary on the Ten Commandments in Deuteronomy,[7] Ramban takes exception to Rambam's opinion. Ramban maintains that Shabbath commemorates Creation alone. Resting on Shabbath and observing its laws are intended only to convince us that God created the universe. The drama of the exodus is merely proof of this truth. The very fact that we were redeemed from Egypt by means of miracles, which disrupted all the laws of nature, proves that there is a power holding dominion over those laws. Thus, according to Ramban, the concept of Shabbath is one: God created the universe. The reference to the exodus in Deuteronomy is intended merely to corroborate this concept and belief.

There is a fascinating difference of opinion between Rambam and Ramban regarding the essence of the festival of Succoth. Rambam, again in *Guide for the Perplexed*,[8] sees Succoth as the festival commemorating Israel's entry into the land after forty years of wandering in the wilderness. For this reason, claims Rambam, all kinds of vegetation become articles of festive celebration and ritual observance. It is as though we are expressing our thanks to God for having brought us out of a barren wilderness into a fruitful land. This is Succoth.

Ramban,[9] however, understands the Succoth festival as celebrating Creation. The seven days of Succoth, he points out, parallel the seven days of Creation, while the eighth day is equated with Israel — the mate of Shabbath — in the mystical, midrashic view of the Creation drama. Additionally, the four species are intended to demonstrate repentance for Adam's sin of eating the forbidden fruit in the Garden of Eden. Finally, the fact that sacrifices are offered on Succoth in the name of seventy nations, comprising all humanity, again underlines the connection between the festival of Succoth and Creation.

The Torah's command to dwell in booths in order to commemorate those in which the Jews lived during their journey through the wilderness,[10] according to Ramban, is merely evidence of Creation, which is being celebrated, just as the exodus from Egypt is evidence of Creation. This is Ramban's view of the festival of Succoth.

Yet, if our formulation of Ramban's view is correct, we must explain why two festivals are necessary to corroborate Creation. For, according to Ramban, both Shabbath and Succoth commemorate Creation.

The principle of Creation contains two elements: first, the

act of Creation itself — *"creatio ex nihilo"*; second, the start of a dynamic process of growth and development both in a physical, material sense and in an idealistic, spiritual sense. By observing Shabbath, we demonstrate two beliefs: First, God created the universe from nothing, formed it according to His will, and, by means of His word, gave existence to all that exists. Second, at the moment of Creation, a dynamic process was effected — a process that includes the perpetual revelation of the forces of nature, man's discovery of them, his utilization of them for his benefit and welfare, his constantly increasing knowledge of God, and his development into nations. It is these historic dynamics that will lead to the Messianic order and the End of Days.

Creation, then, is both an act and the initiation of a process. Evidence of the *act* of Creation is provided by the exodus, with its suspension of the laws of nature, which proves that these laws were created and therefore can be suspended at the will of the Creator. The *process* initiated by Creation, however, is demonstrated by the Succoth festival, which additionally commemorates Adam's transgression and subsequent repentance. This concept is supported by the experiences of the Israelites in the wilderness, a tremendous thrust toward the Messianic era. Succoth, then, offers evidence that this dynamic process was indeed initiated through a Divine act of Creation. Shabbath, though, combines both elements of Creation.

One fairly obvious idea seems to emerge from our discussion. In the act of Creation, only God operates, but in the process initiated by Creation, God invites man to be His partner. Hence the phrase "which God created to make,"[11] which implies that God's act of Creation commences a process in which man actively participates.

Shabbath, therefore, is a source of *kedushah*, holiness, and man merely stands by and beholds the marvel of the act of Creation. It is also a source of *brachah*, blessing, involving man directly and drawing him magnetically as a participant in the unfolding of the immense potential of the dynamic process of Creation.

1. Rashi, Gen. 2:3.
2. Ramban, Gen. 2:1.
3. Gen. 2:1.
4. Exod. 20:11.
5. Deut. 5:15.
6. Pt. II, ch. 31.
7. Ramban, Deut. 5:12.
8. Pt. III, ch. 31.
9. Ramban, Lev. 23:36, 40.
10. Lev. 24:42-43.
11. Gen. 2:3.

פרשת נח
Parashath Noach

Monument to Survival

ויהי כל הארץ שפה אחת ודברים אחדים.
"ALL THE WORLD WAS OF ONE LANGUAGE AND FEW WORDS."
(Genesis 11:1)

This verse introduces one of the more mysterious episodes in the Torah, that of the Tower of Babel. While the sinful acts of the generation of the flood are explicit in the Bible, Midrashic tradition shrouds the wickedness of this generation in mystery.[1] However, a careful examination of select verses and key phrases, coupled with special attention to some rather exciting midrashic suggestions quoted by Rashi, may help disperse the mystery.

Commenting on the phrase "*ud'varim achadim* — and few words," Rashi quotes two midrashic interpretations.[2] One understands the word "*achadim*" to mean "against *Echad*" — against "the One," i.e., God. The other suggests that "*achadim*" may mean "*chadim* — sharp." The meaning of "sharp" words is spelled out by the Midrash: "The earth is destroyed by flood every 1,656 years." The people's plan, therefore, was to build some kind of support that would strengthen the physical structure of the earth. These interpretations are particularly striking because of their remarkable naiveté. But let us continue our analysis.

Verses 3 and 4 appear to be in the wrong order. Verse 3 describes the people's decision to make bricks and burn them thoroughly, and their successful manufacturing of the bricks to replace stone. Verse 4 then describes their decision to build a city and a tower. Logic would dictate that they first decided to build a city and a tower and then, out of necessity, manufactured bricks to implement their decision. The strange order of these two verses calls for some explanation.

Indeed, because of this peculiar sequence, Sforno states that the two verses may have no relation to each other.[3] One, he says, refers to the idea of the people making bricks or building homes. The other refers to the decision of the political leaders to build a city and strengthen the governmental structure via some form of dictatorship. In response to this same difficulty, Netziv suggests that the first *pasuk* alludes to the building of the furnace into which Avraham was thrown for his "heretical" views.[4] This drama, often spoken of in Midrashic literature,[5] is not mentioned in the Bible, and Netziv would therefore like to detect some reference to it in this verse.

The expression in verse 4, "and we shall make a name for ourselves," is somewhat vague. What exactly did the people want to accomplish with this tower and city? There seems to be an urgency here that requires some clarification. It is self-evident that this is the verse in which one should seek the secret of the people's transgression, for it is followed immediately by God's concern and reaction. Furthermore, the confusion of languages is a very curious response on the part of God. While the people's sin is not clear, their punishment is even more peculiar.

We must examine all these circumstances within the context of the historic events of the time, for when one begins to look at this episode carefully, it suddenly appears far from naive or primitive. Indeed, these people may have expressed themselves in rather simple language, but the issues in which they were involved are fundamental moral and theological contentions that are as real today as they were then, touching upon problems that have shaken the very foundations of religious belief.

The flood and its destruction must have been fresh in the minds of the people, having happened only about two hundred years before. Mankind's mood seems to have been one of fatalism bordering on despair, and it emanated from a belief that destruction is inevitable. Tragedy, people thought, was an integral part of life that could not be overcome; ravagement was essential to the architecture of the universe. But here two distinct approaches become apparent:

The religious motif is reflected in the view of God as the destructive force. God destroys, God brings tragedy, God is the vicious annihilator of human life, and every so often He amuses Himself by destroying His creatures. Forgotten are the act of Creation, the graciousness of God's blessings, and the good that comes from the earth for the benefit of man. All the warmth of nature is forgotten. The joy of vegetation, the promise of growth, the sunshine, and the rain are all forgotten. God is viewed as the Divine destroyer. These are the words "against *Echad*" to which Rashi alludes. Perhaps for this reason, throughout this Biblical episode, God is referred to as "*Hashem*."[6] This name of God connotes mercy, whereas "*Elokim*" connotes the cold and objective measure of justice. Indeed, the people's argument against a cruel, destructive God is countered subtly, by the repeated reference to *Hashem*, the God who is gracious and compassionate.

While the people's misperception of God may have been an element of their transgression, it certainly was not their full sin. For the reaction to tragedy cannot be complacency and blind acceptance; the *avoth* (the patriarchs) also challenged God on this issue.[7] The people's transgression must be sought in their tone and in the conclusion they drew from their arguments. However, the religious outlook outlined above was not the only one they expressed.

A second attitude they exhibited was their mechanistic

view of the natural world: There is no God. It is within nature to destroy itself, and, once every thousand years, the structure of the world gives way, and devastation follows.

This second viewpoint may even be more compatible with the concept of God. A creator who exterminates his creation can hardly exist. If there is a Creator, then destruction cannot be His doing. And if extermination and tragedy are inevitable, then better to do away with the concept of God. These are Rashi's "sharp" words.

Confronted with tragedy, particularly its apparent inevitability, man seeks two answers to his dilemma. First, he attempts to fortify this world as much as possible. He begins to apply his genius to perfecting nature. In a primitive way, man wants to try his hand at the herculean task of strengthening the foundations of the world in order to forestall another natural tragedy. Making bricks is merely an example of the feverish activity that must have taken place in a bold venture to prevent another flood.

But this is not all. Man recognizes that, despite all his efforts to perfect the world, despite applying all his skills to averting another tragedy, he can hardly be certain of succeeding. In the face of the formidable and destructive forces of the physical world, it is doubtful whether man can avert a recurrence of this tragedy. But at least there is one thing man can do: He can prevent his own extinction. The building of the tower, then, is an attempt to construct something that will outlive tragedy. If tragedy is inevitable, if this generation is again doomed to extinction, it will at least leave something to be salvaged. The tower will be an eternal reminder of this noble generation, which tried to survive — and did through its monument. This is the "name" the people were seeking.

There are genuine philosophical problems in this episode, and we cannot embark here on a full-length discussion of the Torah's attitude to tragedy. But one thing is certain: The Torah's view of tragedy is not one of defeatism or fatalism, as expressed by this generation. One must grow through the crucible of adversity. Tragedy should promote personal development. The act of confusing tongues was perhaps an attempt to cut off communication so that introspection might produce some kind of spiritual tower more enduring than a tower of brick.

And, indeed, at this point in history, the spiritual tower of Avraham began to appear.

1. *Gen. Rabbah* 38:6.
2. Rashi, Gen. 11:1.
3. Sforno, Gen. 11:3-4.
4. *Ha'amek Davar*, Gen. 9:3.
5. See Rambam, *Mishneh Torah*, "*Hilchoth Avodath Kochavim*" 1:3.
6. Gen. 11:6ff.
7. Note Gen. 18:23.

פרשת לך לך
Parashath Lech Lecha

The Lonely Way

ויאמר ה' אל אברם לך לך מארצך וממולדתך ומבית אביך אל הארץ אשר אראך.
"GOD SAID UNTO AVRAM, 'YOU SHALL GO FROM YOUR LAND, FROM YOUR BIRTHPLACE, AND FROM YOUR FATHER'S HOUSE TO THE LAND THAT I WILL SHOW YOU.'" (Genesis 12:1)

Several expressions in our *pasuk* demand our immediate attention. The phrase *"lech lecha* — you shall go" is, at least according to some commentaries, unique. Rashi explains that the seemingly redundant word *"lecha"* actually implies "for your own good."[1] The Divine dictate therefore implies that Avram shall go forth for his own good, benefiting greatly by following God's command. In contrast, Ramban sees nothing unusual in the phrase *"lech lecha"* and points to many examples of this form.[2] As Netziv[3] notes, Ramban did not have to go far to prove that the phrase *"lecha"* is common: The same form is used at the *akeidah*, where it hardly means "for your own good." Thus, Ramban concludes that the word *"lecha"* signifies nothing.

"El ha'aretz asher ar'eka — to the land that I will show you" is another phrase that must be examined. Here the problem is not linguistic but contextual. Rashi suggests simply that the location of this land is withheld to enhance its desirability.[4] This secrecy probably arouses great interest and awe in Avram. Ramban proposes two interpretations of the phrase

25

"that I will show you."[5] One is that Avram does not know the identity of the land, so he travels from place to place until God appears and identifies it.[6] The other is that Canaan is already mystically known to Avram as a land of special sanctity, so he goes straight there, as the Torah indeed implies.[7] In the second communication, God merely offers further identification and promises. This question of whether Avram already knows the identity of the land prompts Sforno to understand "to the land" as "to that part of the land that I will show you."[8] It also prompts Ibn Ezra to suggest that the command given in chapter 12, verse 1, preceded the story related in chapter 11, which tells of Avram and his family, leaving Ur Kasdim and going to Canaan.[9]

Classic commentaries[10] also note that the phrases "from your land, from your birthplace, and from your father's house" are in the wrong order. For a man leaves his home first and then his land. Here the reverse is indicated.

Using the text itself, we can reconstruct the whole story on the basis of one assumption: The command recorded in chapter 12, verse 1, came to Avram at different times, although the Torah presents it as one statement. After all, Rashi points out that at the beginning of Leviticus, after each Divine order to Moshe, he had time for contemplation and meditation, even though the entire section is introduced by one phrase: "[God] called unto Moshe; God spoke to him from the Tent of Meeting, saying."[11] We suggest similarly that the command to Avram, though recorded in one verse, was given piecemeal.

While Terach's family was still in Ur Kasdim, laboring under the difficulties caused by Avram's strange belief in one, invisible God, God directed Avram to leave his land and birthplace. Simultaneously, Terach decided to leave the area where one of his sons had died and another, Avram, was constantly threatened by the ruling powers. That Terach's decision should coincide with the Divine order to Avram is

The Lonely Way

not at all unlikely. It merely emphasizes that God often reveals Himself within everyday life. Furthermore, this suggestion explains the strange expression "they went out with *them*,"[12] after the verse has already indicated that it was Terach who took the family. While Terach seemingly moved his family for his own reasons, Avram was also a motivating force, although not such an obvious one. He was responding to the Divine directive, which, as we have said, coincided with his family's decision.

Only when the clan settled in Charan did God order Avram to leave his father's house. Avram then headed for Canaan, which apparently was the family's original destination.

This reading resolves the entire difficulty. For the word "*lecha*" becomes very significant — it implies that Avram must go by himself, completely breaking with his family. And God promises that if he does so, He will show him the land, make him into a great nation, and bestow upon him all the blessings stated.

Avram, however, fails to fulfill God's command. He does leave his father's home, detach himself from his family (reestablishing ties only after the *akeidah*),[13] and travel to the land of Canaan — known to him by virtue of either mystical knowledge, God's first order, or the coincidence of Terach's decision to move there just as God instructs Avram to leave his homeland. But he takes Lot with him, contrary to the Divine command. Perhaps Avram hopes to influence him. Nonetheless, this is not God's will. Rather, God wants Avram to be isolated, for only then will he be shown the land and given a historic Divine promise.

When Avram comes to Shechem, God tells him, "To your children shall I give this land...."[14] Nothing more is said — hardly a fulfillment of God's promise to show him the land and bless him as specified in the first few verses of our story. Avram builds an altar to "the God who appears to him,"[15] not to the God who keeps His promise.

Later we read of the rift between Avram and Lot and of their parting ways.[16] Avram is now alone. In isolation, he has finally fulfilled the command of *"lech lecha."* God then offers him a complete view of the land and promises it to him and his children.[17] These children will be as numerous as the dust of the earth; they will develop into a great nation. This extensive promise is indeed a fulfillment of "that I will show you."

1. Rashi, Gen. 12:1.
2. Ramban, Gen. 12:1.
3. *Ha'amek Davar*, Gen. 12:1.
4. Rashi, Gen. 12:2.
5. Ramban, Gen. 12:1.
6. Ibid. 12:7.
7. Ibid. 11:31.
8. Sforno, Gen. 12:1.
9. Ibn Ezra, Gen. 12:1.
10. See *Or HaChayim, Ha'amek Davar*, and *Kli Yakar*.
11. Rashi, Lev. 1:1.
12. Gen. 11:31.
13. See *Ha'amek Davar*, Gen. 22:20.
14. Ibid. 12:7.
15. Ibid. 12:1-3.
16. Ibid. 13:7.
17. Ibid. 13:14-17.

פרשת וירא
Parashath VaYeira

Man's Struggle for Justice

ויגש אברהם ויאמר האף תספה צדיק עם רשע.
"Avraham drew near and said: 'Will you destroy the righteous with the wicked?'" (Genesis 18:23)

This *pasuk* introduces Avraham's celebrated appeal on behalf of Sodom. But more than an appeal, it represents a searching analysis of God's justice. At the very outset, Avraham is disturbed by the possibility of the righteous suffering with the wicked.

Note that Avraham's argument is divided into four parts. First he pleads the case of Sodom — fifty righteous people can be found in this society. Following God's reply, Avraham tries a new tack, seeking Divine mercy for forty-five righteous people. That this approach is new is indicated by Avraham's introduction, "Behold, I want to speak to my God...."[1] His plea on behalf of Sodom if forty righteous people are found is a further innovation, introduced by the phrase "he continued to speak to Him more."[2] The question of thirty seems to fall into the same category as forty, for there is no introduction other than Avraham's urging that God curb his anger. The questions about twenty and ten righteous follow the same introductory pattern as forty and thirty, however, implying that they constitute a fourth category. These categories are deliberate and should be examined in the context of the overall problem of Divine justice and retribution.

First, though, several additional observations are in order.

God replies differently to each category. In the case of fifty, He promises to bear the city's transgression.[3] To the question of forty-five, God responds that He will not destroy the society, but there is no indication of pardon.[4] With regard to forty or thirty, God simply says, "I will not do...,"[5] a strange expression indicating neither pardon nor destruction. And in the case of twenty or ten, God reverts to the phrase "I will not destroy."[6]

Apparently, there are four possibilities: 1) God will destroy Sodom if not even ten righteous persons can be found. 2) God will not destroy the society but will punish it for its crimes if there are forty-five, twenty, or as few as ten righteous people. 3) God will remain passive if there are forty or thirty righteous people. 4) God will pardon Sodom if fifty righteous persons are found.

All this is intended to demonstrate Divine justice, as two more observations will make clear.

First of all, when pleading for forty-five people, Avraham says, "...and I am dust and ashes."[7] Based on a Midrash, Rashi explains that Avraham meant he was almost turned into dust in his struggle against the kings in the war described in Genesis 14, and he was almost burned to ashes when Nimrod threw him into the furnace for preaching about God.[8] How do these incidents relate to our episode, however, and why does Avraham utilize this argument only in the case of forty-five?

Second, our exchange ends, "God departed when He'd finished speaking to Avraham...."[9] This rather dramatic conclusion seems to imply something deep.

I believe that several principles underlie this attempted definition of justice in Divine terms.

First, man must uproot a corrupt society. The struggle against evil is one of the historic responsibilities weighing heavily upon human shoulders. In keeping with our free will, God steps in, so to speak, only after all other possibilities

Man's Struggle for Justice

have been exhausted. Far be it from us to suggest that we have penetrated the unfathomable; the ways of God remain a mystery. But man's obligations can hardly be relegated to the same area of the unknown. The battle against corruption is primarily ours.

Second, a wicked society can have merit on one of two counts. If its very corruption has produced an organized righteous response, this society has almost earned its keep. Alternatively, the mere fact that virtuous men exist in such a society — even if, rather than countering evil, they simply exemplify goodness — is to the evil majority's credit.

Needless to say, these two possibilities differ greatly. In the first case, the society inspired active opposition to its turpitude. In the second case, one can merely commend the corrupt for letting the righteous be, though they hardly constitute a driving force.

Fifty people and forty-five differ just by five. According to Rashi,[10] fifty people means five righteous congregations, one in each of Sodom's five cities. Fifty means that, within each city, a community is dedicated to good and struggling against evil. And when man shoulders his responsibility to develop uprightness and contest depravity, God not only steps aside but offers pardon, for the forces of good will ultimately triumph.

Forty-five means that the just can live in that degenerate society, but their sense of community is lacking. There is no clear response to or dramatic battle against evil. Recalling that, in his own struggles against evil, he was almost destroyed — first by Nimrod and then by the kings — Avraham pleads with God to recognize the herculean strength necessary to wage continuous war on a corrupt society.

God replies that the society's tolerance of the virtuous will stand it in good stead. It will not be destroyed. But punishment is inevitable, since man himself will never overturn this society and eradicate its evil.

In short, an organized *tzibbur*, or public, can be left on its own to defeat evil. Individuals, in contrast, may save society from destruction, but God's retributive intervention is inescapable.

The forty and thirty remain a problem. In these cases, according to Rashi, most cities have communities that challenge evil — most but not all. Will this majority of cities eventually turn the tide? Not necessarily. Therefore, God says, "I will not do." He waits to see what will happen. Perhaps the majority's meaningful reactions to iniquity will spawn a movement. But perhaps not. Meanwhile, there will be neither pardon nor punishment — only a waiting period, with man retaining his precious free will and freedom of action.

The twenty and ten righteous present more definitive circumstances. Such a minority can hardly overturn its corrupt society. The merit of the righteous precludes society's destruction, but ideological revolution is also precluded, so punishment is in order.

What is remarkable about the whole story is that the basic moral issue is never resolved, for if there are fewer than ten upright persons, Sodom — and apparently the righteous within it — will indeed be destroyed. Avraham's question at the outset of his discussion with God, "Will You destroy the righteous with the wicked?"[11] remains.

Hence this episode's strange ending: "God departed when He'd finished speaking to Avraham...."[12] For God's ways are departed from us, shrouded in eternal mystery.

1. Gen. 18:27.
2. Ibid. 18:29.
3. Ibid. 18:26.
4. Ibid. 18:28.
5. Ibid. 18:29.
6. Ibid. 18:31.
7. Ibid. 18:27.
8. Rashi, Gen. 18:27.
9. Gen. 18:33.
10. Rashi, Gen. 18:24.
11. Gen. 18:23.
12. Ibid. 18:33.

פרשת חיי שרה
Parashath Chayei Sarah

Sarah's Influence

ויהיו חיי שרה מאה שנה ועשרים שנה ושבע שנים שני חיי שרה.
"SARAH'S LIFE WAS ONE HUNDRED YEARS AND TWENTY YEARS AND SEVEN YEARS; THESE WERE THE YEARS OF SARAH'S LIFE."
(Genesis 23:1)

Rashi and Ramban both comment at length on the unusual structure of this verse. Rashi takes the repetition of the word "years" as the basis of the rabbinic lesson that Sarah was as sinless at one hundred as she was at twenty and as beautiful at twenty as she was at seven.[1] He thus explains the final phrase, "the years of Sarah's life," as simply summarizing this idea.

In contrast, finding nothing unusual in the repetition of the word "years," Ramban views the final phrase as the basis of the rabbis' teaching that all Sarah's years were equally good.[2]

This phrase is difficult for all the commentators. We should like to translate it very simply, predicated upon some rather obvious considerations.

Avraham and Sarah both actively preached the existence, justice, and righteousness of God. Their mission, as described in Midrashic literature[3] and alluded to repeatedly in the Torah, was to influence people to believe in one invisible, living God who commands man to act justly and kindly. Yet, Avraham and Sarah operated on different levels.

Sarah's Influence

According to the Midrash — as Rashi quotes[4] — Avraham was subordinate to Sarah in prophecy. This means, Netziv suggests, that while Avraham was certainly the prophet *par excellence*, and Sarah could hardly compare with him in that area, her *ruach hakodesh* was superior.[5] This contention requires some explanation.

Prophecy relates to the future and waits upon Divine communication. Rambam insists that although moral and intellectual perfection are required of prophets, they still depend upon God for prophetic wisdom.[6] On the other hand, *ruach hakodesh* is a special sensitivity to the present and need not involve Divine communication. A kind person dedicated to God simply sees life as the unfolding of God's will and interprets existence in Divine terms. Therefore, writes Rambam, prophecy requires the will of God, but *ruach hakodesh* does not.[7]

Avraham excelled in prophecy, so his bases of operation were intellectual activity and prophetic experience. Sarah excelled in *ruach hakodesh*, so her bases of operation were a sensitive soul and the realities of charity and *chessed*. It may further be suggested that Beer Sheva was Sarah's domain. This center of kindness and compassion was of her making. This is where she operated and where her influence was felt. Chevron was Avraham's area of activity. There he prophesied and realized the covenant. There he preached and conducted his intellectual efforts.

Ramban points out[8] that Beer Sheva was a sacred place of prayer for Avraham. After the binding of Yitzchak, Avraham goes there to thank God for sparing his son's life. But Sarah remains in Chevron and dies there.

Perhaps while Avraham honored Sarah's domain in Beer Sheva and transformed it into a house of prayer, Sarah paid homage to Avraham's domain in Chevron and made that a center of prayer. In their love for one another, Avraham is attracted to Beer Sheva, the symbol of Sarah's contribution, while Sarah is drawn to Chevron, the emblem of Avraham's life's work. In any event, they operated on different levels but to one end: to preach the existence of God and the primacy of *chessed*.

Amazingly, after Sarah's death, the entire *parashah* reflects her influence. Her life inspires everyone. Her actions strike deep roots not only within her home but outside it. Her influence even reaches foreign lands. But it is all Sarah.

Let us give a few examples. Scripture tells us that Avraham aged and God blessed him "*bakol* — with everything."[9] This word creates great confusion in Midrashic literature (note Rashi's interpretation[10]). In one of his many mystical adventures, Ramban notes that "*bakol*" is somehow related to *chessed*.[11] Avraham, the personification of the intellectual pursuit of truth, is now blessed with overwhelming *chessed* inherited from Sarah. It is clear from the test Eliezer puts to Rivkah that Avraham seeks a kind, compassionate wife for his son. Indeed, compare the Biblical descriptions of Rivkah providing water for Eliezer and his camels[12] and Avraham providing food for his guests.[13] There is an excitement, a charged atmosphere, a quickened tempo in both cases, indicating that one is influenced by the other. Apparently, even from afar, Rivkah must have heard of her relations and, through her teachers, of Sarah's exemplary life, which she must have studied.[14] Indeed, at almost every step in this story, Sarah is emulated.

The actor may be Avraham, but the spirit is Sarah's; the participant may be Eliezer, but the spirit is Sarah's; the dispenser of *chessed* may be Rivkah, but the driving force is Sarah. When Yitzchak marries Rivkah and brings her into the tent, again Sarah appears — her spirit dominates, her influence permeates every corner of the tent, as beautifully described in Rashi.[15]

Furthermore, take an occasion when Avraham and Sarah did not see eye to eye. When Sarah sensed Yishmael's poten-

Sarah's Influence

tial influence on her son, Yitzchak, she demanded that Avraham send his other son away. Once more it was Sarah's sensitivity that perceived the long-range effect of a continued relationship between the two young men. Avraham was disturbed. Only at God's urging did he accept Sarah's decision and act in accord with her *ruach hakodesh*. And even after Sarah's death, Avraham continues to do so. Before his own passing, he offers gifts to his other children and sends them away, separating them from Yitzchak lest they establish close relationships with him.[16] Incredibly, the very course of action to which Avraham once objected so strongly is now the one he follows so naturally. Again, the influence and spirit of Sarah prevail.

It seems to me that the expression "the years of Sarah's life," which caused so much difficulty, can be interpreted very simply. In this verse, the Torah tells us essentially three things. First, Sarah lived for 127 years. Second, during these years, she excelled in *chessed*. Thus, the phrase, "Sarah's life was..." is not just a statement about physical existence, it alludes to spiritual vitality — Sarah lived throughout her 127 years of existence.

Third — and most important — during these years, Avraham also operated in his unique way. Sarah functioned in Beer Sheva, and Avraham in Chevron. Sarah focused on *chessed*, Avraham on his prophetic, intellectual pursuits. But whose influence dominated? Whose activity was felt more keenly? Sarah's. Her impact struck deeper roots.

In short, it was Sarah's era. Those years were known as "the years of Sarah's life." And so should they be known throughout history. They are not to be recalled as the years of Avraham; they are to be remembered as the era of Sarah.

1. Rashi, Gen. 23:1.
2. Ramban, Gen. 23:1.
3. Rashi, Gen. 12:5, 21:33.
4. Ibid., Gen. 21:12.
5. *Ha'amek Davar*, Gen. 23:1.
6. *Mishneh Torah*, "*Hilchoth Yesodei HaTorah*" 7:1. Cf. Rabbi M. Krakovsky's *Avodath HaMelech* ad loc.
7. Ibid.
8. Ramban, Gen. 23:2.
9. Gen. 24:1.
10. Rashi, Gen. 24:1.
11. Ramban, Gen. 24:1.
12. Gen. 24:18-20.
13. Ibid. 18:6-7.
14. See the author's *Rays of Jewish Splendor* (New York, 1956), pp. 65-70.
15. Rashi, Gen. 24:67.
16. Gen. 25:6.

פרשת תולדות
Parashath Toledoth

Mother of Nations

ויתרצצו הבנים בקרבה ותאמר אם כן למה זה אנכי ותלך לדרש את ה׳.
"THE CHILDREN MOVED ABOUT AGAINST EACH OTHER WITHIN HER; SHE SAID: 'IF SO, WHY AM I THUS?' — SHE WENT TO INQUIRE OF GOD." (Genesis 25:22)

The drama of Rivkah's pregnancy, her inquiry of God, and His reply combine to form a prognostication of historic significance, which we must analyze accordingly.

When Rivkah begins to suffer unusual pregnancy pains, she asks, "If so, why am I thus?" The phrase itself is extremely vague, and so is its point. Rashi interprets this question to mean: Why was I so anxious to become pregnant and have children?[1] Ramban, in an interpretation much more related to the text, explains the question as: Why am I alive?[2] For if Rivkah cannot to bear children, then her life is meaningless and worthless. This explanation appears somewhat simpler, yet it also leaves much of the purpose of the question outside the text itself.

It should further be noted that, before the description of this pregnancy, Rivkah's genealogy is recorded once again. The text relates that she comes from Aram and is the daughter of Bethuel and the sister of Lavan of Aram.[3] According to Rashi, this repetition of Rivkah's family tree indicates her character: She retained her righteousness although her sur-

39

rounding influences were hardly favorable to someone of such personality. One supposes that since this is the beginning of the story of Yitzchak and his family, his wife's character and background could very well deserve repetition.

When Rivkah finally questions the prophet, she receives a fairly long answer: "Two nations are in your womb...and one will be stronger than the other, and the elder will serve the younger."[4] The explanation for her unusual pains should simply have been that she was carrying twins. Amazingly, this is not even mentioned in the reply. In fact, it may not even have been suggested. For at the time of birth, the text uses the expression "and behold, there were twins,"[5] which suggests the surprise of novelty. Instead of this simple explanation of Rivkah's pains, she is treated to a rather lengthy description of a historic drama relating to the distant future.

Commenting on the phrase "*shnei goyim* — two nations," Rashi quotes the Midrash, which, on the basis of a strange spelling of the word "nations," suggests that this term alludes to two great men, Antoninus and Rabbi Yehudah HaNasi, who always had radish on their tables.[6] This somewhat odd translation seems to belittle an otherwise historic phrase.

To capture the flavor of this incident and recognize the full historic proportions of the prophecy, one must reinterpret — in the simplest terms — the fundamental question that moved Rivkah to turn to the prophet for Divine instruction. After all, not every personal problem of the patriarchs was presented in this manner for Divine guidance and a prophetic answer.

Many episodes in the lives of the patriarchs can be understood in a new light if one bears in mind that they all knew of the original covenant between God and Avraham. Though Divine promises of the land and a multitude of children constitute the essence of this covenant, perhaps it was also known prophetically that the family would take the form of twelve tribes, as suggested by Midrashic literature and

Mother of Nations

classic commentaries.[7] Many of the patriarchs' actions, observations, and decisions were prompted and guided by Avraham's covenantal legacy — it colored their thinking, directed their reasoning, and influenced them in a variety of ways.

Bearing this in mind, Rivkah's reaction is only natural: As Yitzchak's wife, she is a link in his family's chain, producing offspring who will continue Avraham's lineage in fulfillment of the Divine promise. Thus, when her pregnancy proves unusually difficult and dangerous for her and her offspring, her question becomes very simple: "Why was I chosen?"[8]

Yitzchak must have children as per God's promise. This way, the covenant will begin to unfold upon the stage of history. But why has she been chosen as his wife? What can she contribute? What does she have to offer within the dynamics of the covenant? The most important and elementary contribution she should be making — childbearing — entails such difficulties that she begins to feel perhaps Yitzchak would have done better with another wife. It appears to me that "Why was I chosen?" is by far the simplest translation of Rivkah's query.

A question of this nature, which probes the meaning of a personality within the covenantal framework, deserves some prophetic reply. And that response is particularly fascinating. What is revealed to Rivkah is the substance of the historic drama, with all the interplay that will spell the accomplishment of the covenant. Essentially, the covenant is predicated on two themes: the existence of God and the primacy of *chessed*. These are the two fundamental teachings of Avraham and the two key elements in the spiritual structure of his family.

Rashi's comment about Antoninus and Rabbi Yehudah HaNasi and their tables is neither outlandish nor out of context. A rabbi's table demonstrates his *chessed*. To go to great lengths to provide necessities and even luxuries for guests and the needy at any given time is merely a manifestation of *chessed*. Rabbi Yehudah HaNasi represents Torah and *chessed*: The wisdom of God and the practice of kindness were the two motivating forces in his life.

To actualize the covenant by fulfilling it is not at all simple. It is a process of both triumphs and frustrations, a continual struggle. In a self-centered society, the principle of *chessed* must constantly be defended. In a secular society, the existence of God must be continuously upheld. And with the development of technology and the growing sophistication of society, the struggle becomes all the more difficult.

All of this is presented to Rivkah symbolically in the prophecy of two nations struggling with each other, each seeking dominion, with the final triumph reserved for the younger. She is then told that the historical realization of the covenant involves a struggle for *chessed* and for the acceptance of the existence of God.

Remarkably, this is indeed the proper response to the problem with which Rivkah is grappling. She has been trying to find her own place within this context, to understand her position within this drama, and it is clarified for her in no uncertain terms.

Rivkah herself was apparently a product of this struggle. Her own faith in God and her own *chessed* withstood this contest. She came from a society that was far removed from the principles of *chessed* and the principles of Avraham. Hers was a home of idolatry and self-centered cunning, the antithesis of *chessed*. Her family could hardly have encouraged her faith or her acts of kindness. Young as she was, she must have experienced the very struggle that was to be the major component in the historic mission of Israel. The text deliberately presents Rivkah's genealogy, and Rashi very beautifully notes her struggle against the environmental influences of this family background. Rashi thus underlines the meaning of the Divine response to Rivkah's search for her own identity and place in Avraham's household.

Rivkah's conflicts and triumph over her environment are a projection of the future. For she plants the seeds of meaningful contest and successful struggle for God and *chessed*.

This is the answer to the question "Why have I been chosen?"

1. Rashi, Gen. 25:22.
2. Ramban, Gen. 25:22.
3. Gen. 25:20.
4. Ibid. 25:23.
5. Ibid. 25:24.
6. Rashi, Gen. 25:23.
7. For instance, see Rashi, Gen. 29:34.
8. Sforno, Gen. 25:22, touches on this.

פרשת ויצא
Parashath VaYeitzei

Family Strength

ויקרא לו לבן יגר שהדותא ויעקב קרא לו גלעד.
"LAVAN CALLED IT 'THE STONE-HEAP OF WITNESS,' AND YAAKOV CALLED IT 'GAL-EID.'" (Genesis 35:13)

In examining the covenant between Yaakov and Lavan, recorded at the conclusion of *VaYeitzei*,[1] we must focus on several problems. First, the sequence of this episode appears strange. Following Yaakov's hasty departure from Lavan's house with every intention of returning to his own father's home, Lavan meets him and declares that Yaakov's wives and children are actually his. What are the implications of this assertion now? Furthermore, when Lavan suggests that they seal a covenant, Yaakov hurriedly calls to his menfolk to assist him in piling stones and breaking bread at the site. Again, what is the significance of this act?

Next, a naming game ensues. Lavan calls this strange monument "Yegar Sahadutha — the gathering of [stones?] is witness." Yaakov calls it "Gal-Eid," the Hebrew counterpart of the Aramaic employed by Lavan. Indeed, Halachic literature[2] usually cites this incident as an example of the Torah's use of either Aramaic instead of Hebrew or Hebrew when Aramaic is indicated. However, a careful examination shows that there is much more here than a mere linguistic contest.

The form of Lavan and Yaakov's vow here is also of special interest. Lavan swears in the name of the God of

Family Strength

Avraham and the god of Nachor and their father (possibly an allusion to Terach), while Yaakov swears by the fear of his father, Yitzchak. Here, the implications seem much clearer, but they must be defined more precisely.

Following the vow, Yaakov offers some kind of sacrifice, and he and his menfolk alone partake of it. At the first party, both Lavan's group and Yaakov's may have eaten together, but here Yaakov and his menfolk break bread alone. What kind of feast is this?

Finally, upon leaving his father's house, Yaakov sets up a monument and names it "Beith El — the house of God,"[3] following God's appearance to him in the dream of the ladder. Upon returning home, he erects another monument which he calls "Mitzpah," this following his final confrontation with Lavan.

All these observations suggest a structure of fundamental significance in the development of the family of Israel, as it unfolds through the story of the patriarchs.

Yaakov's hurried departure from Lavan is prompted not by physical considerations alone — although he suffered physical hardships — but primarily by spiritual considerations. Above all, it is recognition of the uniqueness and inherent purity of the family of Avraham that moves Yaakov to flee.

Traditional Jewish thought has always emphasized that a new genealogy begins with Avraham and Sarah. For this reason, Avraham and Sarah can only have children together through Divine intervention. This reality makes the point, in no uncertain terms, that Avraham's children are not technically the grandchildren of Terach. It is a new family and, indeed, a new entity. Similarly, according to our tradition, in bearing children, Rivkah, Leah, and Rachel, are cut off from their past.

Sforno comments that Yaakov's blessing to the children of Yosef — "may my name and the name of my forefathers Avraham and Yitzchak be called upon them" — is intended

45

to exclude Terach and Nachor, thus reemphasizing the uniqueness and purity of his own family.[4]

It appears to me that the confrontation between Lavan and Yaakov in this *parashah* is Lavan's attempt to fuse the two families, with Yaakov stubbornly insisting upon their separation. With this background, let us review the story step by step.

Hurrying back to his father's house, Yaakov is overtaken by Lavan, who asserts that the children are his and in fact they are really one family, so let there be a covenant between them. But a covenant can have one of two implications. Some covenants are made to bring two parties together in cooperation, and some covenants are intended to keep two parties apart. The covenant between God and Avraham is an example of the former.[5] The covenant between Yitzchak and Avimelech is an example of the latter.[6]

When Yaakov hears of the possibility of a covenant, he immediately sets up a pile of stones to indicate that the essence of this covenant is to separate himself from Lavan. To seal the covenant, the two parties break bread together. And here we come to the first contest between them.

Lavan calls the spot Yegar Sahadutha — "the gathering is witness." Perhaps the point here is not so much the gathering of stones, though this is the symbol. The real point is the gathering of the two sides. The gathering of the stones followed by the gathering of the two parties will affirm the fusion of the two families. Yaakov very carefully and deliberately calls it Gal-Eid: The mound is the witness; the barrier is the testimony. He emphasizes that the purpose of this covenant is not to fuse the two groups into one family, as Lavan seems to imply, but to create an insurmountable barrier between them, thereby preserving the purity and uniqueness of the house of Avraham. Having rejected Lavan's interpretation of the covenant, insisting instead upon his own, Yaakov confronts another subtle attempt to fuse the groups.

Family Strength

Lavan vows in the name of the God of Avraham, the god of Nachor, and the god of their father. This is a wily effort to make Yaakov acknowledge Terach as his grandfather and therefore retain some relationship with Lavan. We can further assume that the God of Avraham is mentioned for Yaakov's sake, the god of Nachor for Lavan's sake, and the god of their father to unify the two. How significant Yaakov's response now becomes. He swears by God — by the fear of his father, Yitzchak. By mentioning Yitzchak, Yaakov removes any doubt regarding his intention that the two groups shall be completely separate and his family shall remain isolated, pure, and free of any physical or philosophical entanglements with Lavan.

Incidentally, in light of this analysis, we can better understand the Haggadah's statement that "Lavan sought to uproot everything." Indeed, by attempting to deny Yaakov's family the right to unique, free development, Lavan was trying to uproot every principle implanted by Avraham.

All Lavan's attempts having come to nought, Yaakov now introduces something new. And we rely rather heavily here on the *Meshech Chochmah*, who finds it especially significant that Yaakov makes a second feast — one that includes meat.[7] Ramban maintains that the patriarchs observed *mitzvoth* only in the Land of Israel, not outside it.[8] This is where Yaakov introduces the use of *shechitah*, ritual slaughter, and for good reason. Apart from other rationales that may be suggested for slaughter, *shechitah* and *kashruth* create a spiritual wall between Jew and non-Jew. Yaakov strengthens the established separateness of Israel with a meal involving *shechitah*, to which only his own menfolk are invited. This meal, with all its implications, cements the final severance of Yaakov's family from Lavan's. This is the essential principle of this chapter.

When Yaakov begins his journey to Lavan, he dreams of a ladder, angels, and God's presence,[9] and he sets up a monument and calls the site Beith El, the house of God.

Could it be that, at the conclusion of this section, Yaakov again sets up a monument to commemorate the purity of his family and its separate existence? And one often wonders which is the real house of God, the synagogue or the Jewish family.

1. Gen. 31:43-54.
2. For example, see *Megillah* 9a.
3. Gen.28:19.
4. Sforno, Gen. 48:16.
5. Gen. 15:18.
6. Ibid. 21:32.
7. *Meshech Chochmah*, Gen. 31:54.
8. Ramban, Gen. 26:5.
9. Gen. 28:12.

פרשת וישלח
Parashath VaYishlach

Chariot of God

ויעל מעליו אלקים במקום אשר דבר אתו.
"AND GOD WENT UP FROM HIM AT THE PLACE WHERE HE SPOKE WITH HIM." (Genesis 35:13)

This verse sounds somewhat mystical, but what it means in our own terminology is rather elusive. As a matter of fact, Rashi comments that he does not know the significance of the second phrase of the verse, "at the place where He spoke with him."[1] Sforno suggests that it means God spoke to Yaakov at the same place where He first spoke to him, upon his leaving his father's house on his journey to Lavan.[2]

Ramban notes[3] that the expression "God went up from him" is similar to one found in the case of Avraham.[4] According to Ramban, the phrase implies that this was no mere dream or vision, it was a very real experience of God. Parenthetically, it may be remarked that this wording signifies the moment when both Avraham and Yaakov become *avoth*, patriarchs. In fact, the traditional concept that the patriarchs are "the chariot of Divine glory" is founded upon the expressions noted here.[5]

However, all this commentary still does not explain the meaning of "at the place where He spoke with him." Netziv tries to interpret it in terms of the significance of the special relationship between God and the *tzaddik*, the righteous one, at their place of meeting.[6]

I should like to suggest a simple interpretation of this phrase based on several ideas about the episode described here, particularly Yaakov's name change, which takes place during this revelation.

When one carefully examines the verse in which God changes Yaakov's name to Yisrael, one notes an unusually cumbersome sentence structure, apparently repetitive and almost contradictory: "God said to him, 'Your name is Yaakov; your name will no longer be called Yaakov, but Yisrael will be your name' — He called his name Yisrael."[7]

The phrase "your name is Yaakov" has been interpreted according to Halachah as meaning that the name Yaakov is retained. Whereas, when Avraham's name was changed, his original name was dropped, here the original name, Yaakov, remains. Furthermore, note the repetition: His name will not be called Yaakov; his name will be called Yisrael; He called him Yisrael. A superficial reading of the text reveals an apparent redundancy.

In conjunction with the name change, this passage records a series of Divine promises: "A people and a multitude of peoples shall come from you, and kings shall issue forth from your loins."[8] The meaning of "a people" and "a multitude of peoples" is extremely vague. According to Rashi, these phrases refer to the forthcoming birth of Binyamin and to Menasheh and Ephraim, the children of Yosef, and "kings shall issue forth from your loins" alludes to Shaul and Ishbosheth.[9]

Regarding God's promise of the land, which He invariably couples with the blessing of children, there is also a strange structure: "And the land that I gave to Avraham and to Yitzchak, I will give to you, and to your children after you I will give the land."[10] The repetition of "I will give" seems redundant and in need of explanation.

There seems to be something quite crucial in this epi-

Chariot of God

sode. Something of tremendous historic significance is suggested in this Divine revelation. To appreciate it fully, particularly its historic projection, one would do well to reconstruct the circumstances.

Yaakov is now returning to his father's house. His family is almost complete; only Binyamin remains to be born. The branches of this illustrious family are nearly all full-grown and beginning to function. The dynamics of God's promise to Avraham are about to start operating. The full impact of God's covenant with him, which is to be realized through the suffering in Egypt and the liberation therefrom, will now materialize. More than that, the history of Israel, which begins with the words "your seed shall be a stranger in a land not theirs"[11] and leads to the coming of the Messiah, the final redemption, and the End of Days, begins its dramatic realization very concretely. The family intrigue that leads to the sale of Yosef and the descent into Egypt opens this narrative. On the threshold of this historic moment, God appears to Yaakov and reveals to him the essence of his family history.

From this moment on, Yaakov's experiences reflect the nation of Israel. Israel represents two phenomena: a name and an experience. It is a name expressive of the ideas that the angel related after he struggled unsuccessfully with Yaakov.[12] It is an experience expressing the historic truth that God directs the history of this people, He is intimately related to it, and His hand can be seen in the unfolding history of nations generally but especially with regard to Israel. The name of God is identified with Yaakov and his family. Therefore, when God changes Yaakov's name to Yisrael, He does two things: He gives him the name Yisrael, and He relates the Yisrael experience to his family, which becomes God-directed in every sense: social, political, and historical.

This duality explains the repetition we pointed out earlier. The first phrase, "Your name will no longer be called Yaakov, but Yisrael will be your name," alludes to the Yisrael experience. "He called his name Yisrael" is the technical application of a given name.

Having conveyed this idea, God proceeds to present a breathtaking image of Israel's history: "A people and a multitude of peoples...." There is a dimension here that one can sense in the music of the text if not in the text itself: There will be different periods in the history of this family. First, it will be forged into one nation, united under the kingdom of God. Following the liberation from Egypt, the revelation and the ensuing *midbar* (desert) experience will chisel out one people united under the banner of God, a unification eventually realized in the land of their fathers, with the Temple in Jerusalem as the symbol of that unity under God. This is the meaning of "a people."

But the history of Israel will fluctuate, its fortunes will change, and there will be times of dispersion. The "people" will turn into "a multitude of peoples" driven from their land and into the lands of their exile. But they will be reunited as a congregation through the unifying forces of Torah and Jewish nationhood. This is "a multitude of peoples." "A people" and "a multitude of peoples" are ways of expressing the ups and downs of Israel's history. Ultimately, however, kings will issue forth, and the Messiah will appear to offer eternal redemption in the End of Days.

When God turns to the matter of the land, He says, "...I will give [it] to you, and to your children after you I will give the land." We have already noted the repetition here. But it is quite deliberate and meaningful, underlining the historic fact that the act of giving will be repeated several times. I will give it to you once, God insists, and I will give it to you again after the dispersion and again until the final, ultimate redemption.

There is something rather fascinating about the two events that follow this Divine communication to Yaakov, which we have analyzed from a historic perspective: Binyamin is born,

Chariot of God

and Yaakov constructs Rachel's tomb. Binyamin is known in our literature as "the host of Divine glory." Indeed, in his territory, on the Temple mount, God's presence was found.[13] Rachel's tomb is traditionally situated on the road the Israelites traveled when they were driven into exile in Babylon.[14]

The birth of Binyamin therefore foreshadows the ultimate realization of "a people." The tomb of Rachel foreshadows the dispersion of "a people" into "a multitude of peoples." Viewed from the historic perspective we have adopted as our guideline, the Divine communication to Yaakov and the two personal events that follow become united, integrated into a single drama.

We now interpret the text whose meaning has eluded us in the simplest terms. "God went up from him at the place where He spoke with him" is intended as a limitation. God left Yaakov only at the place where He spoke with him. The Divine communication was completed, but the intimate relationship between God and Yaakov was hardly finished. In fact, it was just beginning. Bearing the name Yisrael and constantly subjected to the experience suggested in the concept of this name, Yaakov indeed undergoes the tragedies and glories of his history as the chariot of God.

God went up from him but only at the place where He spoke with him. In reality, in historic terms, God has remained with Yaakov eternally.

1. Rashi, Gen. 35:13.
2. Sforno, Gen. 35:13.
3. Ramban, Gen. 35:13.
4. Gen. 17:22.
5. Ramban, Gen. 35:13.
6. *Ha'amek Davar*, Gen. 35:13.

7. Gen. 35:10.
8. Ibid. 35:11.
9. Rashi, Gen. 35:11.
10. Gen. 35:12.
11. Ibid. 15:13.
12. Ibid. 32:29.
13. Deut. 33:12 (note Rashi).
14. Rashi, Gen. 48:7.

פרשת וישב
Parashath VaYeishev

THE INHERITANCE

אלה תלדות יעקב....
"THESE ARE THE GENERATIONS OF YAAKOV...."   (Genesis 37:2)

This statement opens the whole story of the conflict among the children of Yaakov, which results in the sale of Yosef and, ultimately, the descent of the family into Egypt. As such, it has given rise to a great deal of comment by the classic interpreters of our Torah.

This is not the first time such a statement appears. It is used with Noach — "These are the generations of Noach..."[1] — and Yitzchak — "And these are the generations of Yitzchak the son of Avraham...."[2] It always presents a problem, and I should like to formulate that problem in the clearest terms.

In its simplest form, the word *toledoth* — commonly translated as "generations" — refers to children. As a matter of fact, when the Torah states, "This is the book of the generations of Adam...,"[3] it simply pertains to children, with the subsequent recitation of generations supporting this interpretation. Similarly, the phrase "And these are the generations of the children of Noach..."[4] is followed by an enumeration of generations of children and grandchildren.

However, our text and the texts referring to the *toledoth* of Noach and Yitzchak present a special difficulty: they are not followed by names of children.

55

The Depths of Simplicity

Rashi insists that the translation of the word *toledoth* is always "children,"[5] and, wherever this term is not followed by an enumeration of children, something must be interpolated in the text. In the case of Noach, the digression of "Noach was a righteous man; he was perfect in his generations..." accords with the principle that any mention of the righteous demands an expression of blessing. In the case of Yitzchak, the term *toledoth* refers to Yaakov and Eisav, though the Torah begins with the marriage of Yitzchak to Rivkah, her genealogy, and the unique birth of her twins.

Concerning our text, Rashi is hard put to find an explanation, for the children have already been born and are not enumerated in the subsequent verse. He therefore inserts the word "of" and renders the text: "These are [the episodes] of the generations of Yaakov." Thus, Rashi retains the fundamental meaning of the term *toledoth*.

Ibn Ezra maintains that *toledoth* may refer to events.[7] The word therefore introduces significant occurrences in the life of Noach, Yitzchak, or Yaakov, as the case may be.

Ramban interprets *toledoth* here much as Rashi interprets it in the case of Yitzchak.[8] "These are the generations of Yaakov" refers to Yosef and his brethren, the protagonists of the subsequent Torah sections. Furthermore, Ramban suggests that the phrase may refer to all seventy of Yaakov's immediate offspring, who are indeed enumerated, though their enumeration is interrupted by certain incidents.

Regarding this problem, we find a famous comment by Rashbam, in which he advocates simple interpretation and translates this phrase almost as Ramban does.[9]

The problem is clear, and most commentaries have difficulty supplying a simple and definitive translation. We should like to approach the problem somewhat differently, since it is unique. In the case of Noach and Yitzchak, the phrase is employed at the beginning of their careers. Here, it is used in the middle of a story. It introduces neither Yaakov's life nor the birth of his children. For that matter, it does not even introduce his children's activities. The Torah has already recorded their exploits.

We shall preface our theme by examining a *mishnah*, of which we offer a fairly loose translation — "A father endows his son with beauty, strength, wealth, longevity, and the characteristics of the generations before him, and this is the end, the *keitz*."[10] Needless to say, the *mishnah* is quite difficult, and it is worth examining all the commentaries thereon.[11] Nevertheless, permit us the luxury of a somewhat unconventional interpretation (although its basic elements are found in the commentaries):

The conflict between free will and God's will is an age-old problem discussed extensively in most philosophic systems. Rambam and Ramban both address the matter, particularly with regard to the Divine decree that the Egyptians would oppress the children of Avraham and be punished for it.[12] Did not the decree remove the Egyptians' free will? And if so, how can they be punished for their deeds? The solutions are many, but when all is said and done, the difficulty is not really resolved.

What we should like to suggest will not solve the problem. In the final analysis, we shall fall back on Rambam's contention that an adventure such as this involves a conceptual definition of God's knowledge, which is tantamount to defining His essence and therefore beyond man's comprehension.[13]

Our thesis is as follows: There is a *keitz*, an end, a goal, which must be realized. However, the means of reaching that goal remain open and depend upon the uniqueness of the people involved.

The Divine plan will be realized. But God operates, so to speak, through reality, i.e., through the will, tendencies, and character of man. People possess traits; they possess wills and act in keeping with their unique personalities. Their qualities are inherited, which itself limits their freedom of will and movement. God will ultimately accomplish whatever end must be accomplished through man's free will, tendencies, and character.

This is what the *mishnah* suggests. The father endows his son with characteristics that will be reflected in future generations, and the *keitz* — the goal or end — will reflect and be actuated by these tendencies.

The Divine decree expressed to Avraham was clear and unequivocal. "You shall surely know that your seed shall be a stranger in a land not theirs."[14] This goal, this *keitz*, is going to be realized one way or another. One can easily visualize many ways by which Yaakov and his children could have been brought into Egypt. Midrashic tradition asserts that, had it been necessary, Yaakov would have been brought to Egypt in chains.[15] The *keitz*, the fulfillment of God's decree, is beyond question; the means remain open and undefined, depending upon the nature of the personages involved.

What actually happened should be viewed on two levels (the Midrash treats this theme extensively.[16]) On one level, Yaakov's children squabble, jealousy sets in, and a hideous crime is perpetrated: A brother is sold into slavery. As a result, the family is thrown into turmoil and then descends into Egypt to reunite with the lost brother, who has become one of that country's rulers. This is the human level.

On the Divine level, God is, in His own way, fulfilling His decree that the children of Avraham shall be persecuted in a strange land.

But — and this is the point — the way the family is brought into Egypt is in keeping with the characteristics implanted by Yaakov. Jealousy among brothers is already known in this family. The struggle for the rights and privileges of prominence is also not new to this household. As Rashi points out, what happened to Yosef had already happened to Yaakov. What we are trying to say is that not only had it

The Inheritance

already occurred, but these sentiments, these tendencies were part of the nature of these people. And precisely because these characteristics were inherited from the father of this family, the Divine decree unfolded and reached fulfillment in this manner.

This is why the Torah introduces the whole drama of the sale of Yosef and the subsequent descent into Egypt with the phrase "These are the generations of Yaakov...": The events about to be described characterize the children of Yaakov and display what they've inherited from their father.

God's will is accomplished through man's personality and tendencies.

1. Gen. 6:9.
2. Ibid. 25:19.
3. Ibid. 5:1.
4. Ibid. 10:1.
5. Rashi, Gen. 6:9, 25:19.
6. Ibid., Gen. 37:2.
7. Ibn Ezra, Gen. 6:9, 37:1.
8. Ramban, Gen. 37:2.
9. Rashbam, Gen. 37:2.
10. *Eduyoth* 2:9.
11. See Rambam, Bartenura, *Tifereth Yisrael*, etc.
12. Ramban, Gen. 15:13; Rambam, *Mishneh Torah*, "*Hilchoth Teshuvah*" 6:5.
13. Ibid. 5:5.
14. Gen. 15:13.
15. *Gen. Rabbah* 86:1.
16. Ibid. 85.

פרשת מקץ
Parashath MiKeitz

BROTHERLY SPIES

ויזכר יוסף את החלמות אשר חלם להם ויאמר אלהם מרגלים אתם לראות את ערות הארץ באתם.

"YOSEF REMEMBERED THE DREAMS THAT HE HAD DREAMT ABOUT THEM; HE SAID TO THEM, 'YOU ARE SPIES — TO SEE THE NAKEDNESS OF THE LAND HAVE YOU COME.'"

(Genesis 42:9)

The celebrated meeting of Yosef and his brothers and the intrigue he initiates always appear strange and inexplicable. Apart from other difficulties, an ethical problem is involved. How does Yosef take it upon himself to cause so much anguish to his aged father, while the simple act of identifying himself would have spared Yaakov so much pain and suffering? Commentaries suggest that Yosef had to approach the issue of reconciliation with great circumspection lest his reappearance on the scene throw his family into greater turmoil and aggravate, at least psychologically, the already tense household atmosphere.[1] However, this insight hardly answers all the questions and does not solve any real problems.

There are two outstanding opinions regarding Yosef's reaction to his brothers' bowing down to him. Yosef considered this act a realization of his dreams,[2] says Rashi, who hardly deals with the propriety of the young man's action. According to Ramban, on the other hand, Yosef realized that neither of his dreams had been fulfilled.[3] First, only ten of his brothers had paid homage to him. Second, his father had not been among them, and his presence was integral to Yosef's dreams.

Ramban further argues that, had Yosef felt that his dreams had been realized, then the game he played with his brothers — and, by inference, with his father — would have been immoral. Recognizing, however, that his dreams had not been fulfilled, continues Ramban, Yosef made every effort to bring the family down to Egypt to effect this fulfillment.[4]

At first glance, Ramban only serves to intensify the problem, for what gives Yosef the moral right to act as God's agent? If his dreams are indeed some form of prophecy — and this remains to be determined — then God can take care of His plans in His own way. Is it man's province to undertake morally dubious courses of action in order to bring God's will to fruition? Furthermore, what, in fact, is the purpose of fulfilling the dreams? What is accomplished by Yosef's brothers and father bowing to him?

These issues are difficult, to put it mildly. While I wonder whether anything we say can ease their moral impact, let alone resolve them, I should like to suggest one approach to the thinking that may have initiated these events.

At the moment, we will not consider what evidence is needed to attach prophetic significance to a dream. However, if a dream is prophetic, then it must direct the individual toward some course of action. Otherwise, one may ask, "What is the purpose of the revelation altogether?" As a matter of fact, not only is this the thinking of Yosef, but it is a philosophy found throughout the Torah and Midrashic and Talmudic literature. Any confrontation with the Divine involves some directive to man. Any revelation of the Divine places some responsibility on man. It was not only the revelation at Sinai that brought commandments in its wake; even the more mystical revelation of God's attributes is intended to define and mold man's morality.[5]

In short, prophecy is not just informative; it indicates that something must be done. However, except where the Divine directive is clear and unequivocal, man retains his freedom of choice and merely follows Divine direction.

Yosef illustrates this approach. Through dream interpretation, Yosef reveals the butler's eventual release from prison and return to his position in Pharaoh's court. Yosef then suggests that the butler mention him to Pharaoh, thus hastening his own release.[6] Our teachers in the Midrash view this suggestion as a breach in Yosef's reliance upon God.[7] Yet Yosef believed and sought to emphasize that Divine revelations — here in dream form — demand some human response.

Consider Yosef's interpretation of Pharaoh's dreams. Recognizing in them a Divine revelation of Egypt's economic future, Yosef advises Pharaoh on how to meet the approaching famine, structure the country's economy, and prepare for the emergency.[8] Classic commentaries attempt to explain why, although Yosef is asked only to interpret the dreams, he also offers economic advice.[9] But the reason is quite simple: Yosef responds to dreams by taking the initiative. If a dream is some kind of prophecy, it must suggest a directive.

Let us now study Yosef's dreams once more. Yosef had no ambitions to lead his brothers. Perhaps this is why the Torah tells us he was merely a shepherd with them, possibly even subordinate to them.[10] The Torah also notes that Yosef was particularly close to Bilhah and Zilpah's children,[11] indicating his modesty and lack of pretensions to leadership, at least then.

All these considerations are important. Yosef's dream of his brothers' bowing before him can be prophetic only if it cannot be attributed to fantasies emanating from his ambition. Additionally, Yosef may not have recognized any Divine revelation in his dreams until the brothers bowed down to him.

The phrase "Yosef remembered the dreams" suggests very strongly that until then, he had hardly thought about them. Only the sight of his brothers' bowing indicated that the dream was a Divine revelation.

One more consideration is necessary to appreciate the structure of the story. Avraham's prophecy that his children would be enslaved in a strange land[12] was probably well known in his family. Surely his descendants studied his teachings and were constantly mindful of his prophecies. Interestingly, then, before his death, Yosef asks his brothers to take his remains with them when God redeems them from Egypt.[13] And this although the suffering and oppression did not begin until after the death of all the children of Yaakov. Clearly, Yosef, in his dreams, perceives a Divine directive that his rulership was to lure his family down to Egypt. And in his plan, he saw two advantages.

Instead of Yaakov coming in chains, as the Midrash suggests would have been the alternative, Yosef felt he could bring his father to Egypt with dignity. Perhaps Yosef feared that disclosing his identity early would give rise to a feeling among his brothers that he should come with them to visit their father; whereas Yosef realized that his family was destined to come to him.

Furthermore, Ramban implies that Yosef wanted all his brothers *and* his father to bow to him in order to fulfill the dreams completely.[14] For Avraham's children were going to be slaves oppressed by a strange ruler for four centuries. It may be significant that the period of subjection began with prostration not to a stranger but to one of themselves. Perhaps such an act injected them with a feeling of *avduth*, enslavement, first to their own brother, then to a benevolent monarch, and finally to a despot.

All this hardly excuses Yosef's causing his father to suffer. But perhaps it lends some rationale to an episode even stranger in many respects than the sale of Yosef itself.

THE DEPTHS OF SIMPLICITY

1. *Daath Zekeinim*, Gen. 42:1.
2. Rashi, Gen. 42:9.
3. Ramban, Gen. 42:9.
4. Ibid.
5. See *Rosh HaShanah* 17b.
6. Gen. 40:14.
7. *Gen. Rabbah* 89.
8. Gen. 41:33-36.
9. *Or HaChayim*, Gen. 41:33.
10. Gen. 37:2.
11. Ibid.
12. Ibid. 15:13.
13. Ibid. 50:25.
14. Ramban, Gen. 42:9.

פרשת ויגש
Parashath VaYigash

Reconciliation

ויאמר יוסף אל אחיו גשו נא אלי ויגשו ויאמר אני יוסף אחיכם אשר מכרתם אתי מצרימה.

"YOSEF SAID UNTO HIS BROTHERS, 'COME NEAR TO ME'; THEY CAME NEAR; HE SAID, 'I AM YOUR BROTHER YOSEF, WHOM YOU SOLD INTO EGYPT.'" (Genesis 45:4)

Let us direct our attention to the episode that begins with this declaration. In verses 4-8, not only does Yosef reveal himself to his brothers, but he consoles them, speaking with compassion and understanding and seemingly trying to allay his siblings' fears.

But when one examines these few verses, they appear quite repetitious. Let us review them briefly:

In verse 5, Yosef urges his brothers not to be guilt-ridden and angry with themselves for selling him to Egypt, for it was God who sent him as a provider. In verse 6, he then describes the famine and its projected duration.

In verse 7, Yosef reiterates the story, stating that God sent him "to preserve for you a remnant in the land" and to give them life "...for a great deliverance." Why does Yosef repeat that God has sent him? Furthermore, the expressions "to preserve for you a remnant in the land" and "for a great deliverance" deserve careful consideration. They are certainly very difficult to explain.

In verse 8, Yosef seems to start the story all over. Again he tells his brothers that not they but God sent him to Egypt. But he has said this twice already! Interestingly, Yosef also says, "it was not you who *sent* me," not "it was not you who *sold* me." Though the reason for this wording is quite obvious — for they did sell him — I believe that fundamental issues are being treated here.

What we have is, first, a glimpse into Yosef's analysis of the celebrated sale and all its implications, and, second, an analysis of sin and the responsibility it entails.

Let us first clarify the two phrases Yosef utilizes to calm his brothers, "do not despair" and "do not be angry." Transgression may lead to two results: catastrophe and, by some strange turn of events, good fortune.

The latter in no way mitigates an offense. One cannot explain away or rationalize a sin merely by pointing to its result. Man is responsible for his deeds and must carry the burden of his transgressions. Nonetheless, his responses vary with their outcomes: An unfortunate outcome prompts despair, while a fortunate one prompts anger at oneself for transgressing altogether, for the same results may have been realized by other means.

In verses 5 and 7, Yosef endeavors to dispel these two feelings. In verse 5, Yosef states that his brothers need not despair, for the result of their action was good. It could have been tragic, but somehow God made Yosef a provider who would satisfy their needs during the famine. This is his first point.

Yosef then says something along these lines: "There is more to all this. Not only must you not despair, but you must not even experience anger over the sale itself." What he means is that not only did their transgression result in something good, but the very sale — the nature of the sin itself — contained positive elements.

There was tension among the brothers in this family;

there was hatred, as the Torah indicates.[1] The sale and the ultimate reconciliation brought about a love for one another that could otherwise never have been realized. The sale of Yosef, its tragic implications, and Yaakov's suffering all eventually lead to warm brotherhood, sympathy, and compassion. Affection of this sort can result only from such an abhorrent act as the sale of a brother. Its aftermath unites the family as never before.

Once we deal with love, compassion, and understanding within Yaakov's family, we suddenly begin to think in historic terms, for the unity of this family is essential for redemption. This idea can be understood on various levels.

First, tradition has it that the second Temple was destroyed because of hatred between Jews. Redemption will come — says Rabbi Avraham Yitzchak Kook, of blessed memory — through love, compassion, and understanding.[2] Israel's very existence in its land and ultimate redemption are both predicated upon family love and harmony.

Ramban points out that when Yaakov travels to Egypt with his family, he offers *shelamim*, peace offerings, to temper the Divine justice about to appear in full force.[3] While Ramban speaks in highly mystical terms, we may translate this concept into our own parlance. Untempered Divine justice implies that God removes Himself, so to speak, from Israel. Conversely, tempering justice ensures that God is with Israel and suffers with us, so to speak. But Divine reaction mirrors man's deeds. God's involvement with and concern for Israel depends upon our involvement with and concern for each other. Thus, Yaakov offers *shelamim*, gathering his entire family to partake of them and thereby become infused with love and harmony. This bonding, in turn, elicits God's understanding and intervention, for God tells Yaakov that He, too, will go down to Egypt and suffer with them.[4]

In verse 7, the expressions "to preserve for you a remnant in the land" and "for a great deliverance" should not be regarded narrowly, for they have historic import. Yosef is saying that not only has his sale led directly to love and reconciliation, but it establishes Israel's harmony for the future, even until redemption.

Yosef has therefore established two points. First, there should be no despair, for the result of the transgression was positive. Second, the brothers should not be angry with themselves, for their sin itself had positive implications.

But now Yosef comes to the thrust of his argument, which for him is possibly its most painful point. Given the positive results of the transgression and even its intrinsic productive elements, it almost seems as though the sin has been erased. Is there no need for repentance?

Answers Yosef in verse 8, "it was not you who sent me." "Remember," he seems to say, "that you sold me *and* that God sent me." There is no cause for despair, because the outcome has been positive. There should not even be anger among themselves, for the transgression itself has very positive elements. But the brothers should not consider themselves the driving force behind the whole drama. Having heard everything Yosef has said, they may indeed have been overwhelmed by the magnitude of their contribution to the economic rehabilitation of the whole world and to family unity, with all its historic and even cosmic implications. To this misconception, Yosef feels duty-bound to reply that all they have contributed is a transgression. They are not the senders but the sellers.

This sin may not call for despair or anger, but it does call for repentance.

1. Gen. 37:4, 8.
2. *Oroth HaKodesh*, vol. 3, *shaar* 2, *seder* 4, ch. 10.
3. Ramban, Gen. 46:1.
4 Gen. 46:4.

פרשת ויחי
Parashath VaYechi

THE PROVIDER VERSUS ROYALTY

יהודה אתה יודוך אחיך....
"YEHUDAH, TO YOU, YOUR BROTHERS WILL PAY HOMAGE...."
(Genesis 49:8)

With this clear and simple expression, an aged, dying Yaakov finally bestows royalty upon Yehudah. As Ramban explains in great detail, this prophecy means that the monarchy will always remain with the descendants of Yehudah, and all Jewish kings must come from his tribe.[1] In fact, insists Ramban, the Hasmoneans transgressed by appointing one of their priestly family to the throne of Israel, for kingship belongs to Yehudah.

However, Yehudah did not acquire royalty without a struggle. The story of Yosef and his brothers can be read — and must be understood — on several levels, and one level that is often overlooked involves this struggle over royalty. Yehudah and Yosef compete for the throne. In the end, Yosef is defeated and Yehudah triumphs.

Viewed from this perspective, many elements of the story take on highly dramatic proportions, and certain textual difficulties can be resolved. Initially, Yaakov seems inclined to offer the mantle of royalty to Yosef. Thus, no sooner is Yosef born than Yaakov asks Lavan's permission to return to his home. This inclination also explains why Yaakov made his son a coat of many colors[2] and why, upon being sent to visit his brothers in Shechem, Yosef states, "*Hineini* — I am prepared,"[3] a response often reserved for one called upon to perform an historic mission or to assume royalty.

Furthermore, if we bear in mind that Yaakov favored Yosef for royalty, one of the most curious textual peculiarities becomes clear. After Yaakov is renamed Yisrael,[4] the Torah seems to give no instructions about the use of these two names. There is virtually no pattern in their interchangeability. I should like to suggest a simple pattern, citing several striking textual examples. A careful reading of this entire drama will support my theory, with one or two possible exceptions.

"Yaakov" is associated with g*aluth*, exile. "Yisrael" is associated with royalty. (*Sar*, the root of the name, means "ruler," connoting sovereignty and royalty.) Consequently, whenever Yaakov speaks to or about Yosef, or the Torah relates the two, the name suddenly changes to Yisrael. For Yaakov wanted Yosef to have the mantle of royalty. Let me point out two particularly telling examples:

Introducing the story of Yosef and his brothers, the Torah says, "These are the generations of Yaakov...,"[5] and describes the relationship between the brothers. Then suddenly, the Torah states, "And *Yisrael* loved Yosef more than all his [other] sons."[6] Note the change to Yisrael when his relationship to Yosef is involved.

Similarly, "Yaakov lived in the land of Egypt seventeen years, and Yaakov's days, the years of his life, were seven years and forty and a hundred years,"[7] but "The days of *Yisrael* drew near to die; he called his son Yosef."[8] Again, the text speaks of Yaakov, but it is Yisrael who summons Yosef.

The most startling change of this kind, which proves my theory beyond any doubt, occurs after Yosef arrives at his ailing father's bedside: "It was told to Yaakov — he said, 'Behold, your son Yosef is coming to you'; *Yisrael* mustered his strength, he sat on the bed."[9] Clearly, Yosef's appearance prompts the sudden change in name.

Without analyzing the whole story here, suffice it to say that this principle is maintained with amazing consistency.

There is one outstanding deviation, however: "Yaakov said to Yosef...."[10] This is the only encounter between the patriarch and his beloved son in which the name Yaakov is used. But this anomaly, too, supports my theory, for here Yaakov offers Yosef the double portion of the *bechorah*, the birthright, apparently in exchange for the royalty he will not receive. For this reason, the Torah uses the name Yaakov.

When Yehudah approaches the ruler of Egypt, not knowing that it is Yosef, the Midrash depicts this dramatic meeting as a confrontation between two contenders for the throne.[11] Eventually, Yosef himself recognizes his failure. He admits that he has been sent merely as a provider and that all his machinations have been to no avail, for he has not brought his father down to Egypt to bow before him. In fact, Yaakov never bows to Yosef; instead, the patriarch confers royalty upon Yehudah.

Interestingly, both this struggle and its outcome have historic and even eschatological implications. The very fact that Yosef appears at first to triumph and attain royalty, only to be dethroned by Yehudah, has Messianic ramifications.

According to the traditional view of the Messianic era, the Messiah son of Yosef will precede the Messiah son of David. Without indulging in the mysticism of this tradition, the fact is that it follows fairly closely the drama of Yosef's struggle with Yehudah for leadership. But this vision goes even farther than that.

Jewish redemption has its own Divine blueprint, about which we know very little. One need only read the last chapter of Rambam's *Mishneh Torah* and note his insistence that we really do not know much about the advent of the Messiah and the End of Days.

Nonetheless, Ramban comments that certain prophetic phrases in the Torah foretell when Israel will repent, and God will return to His nation.¹² Yet, upon scrutinizing the text, it appears that, even after the Jews attribute all their woes to Divine abandonment, God asserts that He will continue to turn away from them.¹³ This withdrawal, after what appears to be a statement of repentance by the Jewish people, has challenged all Torah commentaries. Ramban offers a most unusual interpretation: When the Jews sin, God will turn away from them both as their King and as their merciful Father. However, following their repentance, although He will still not act as their King and redeem them, He will return, so to speak, with mercy.

Apparently, Ramban visualizes redemption in two stages: first, the return of mercy, and then, the restoration of the kingdom of Heaven, in all its regal splendor, heralding complete salvation. This process parallels the coming of the two Messiahs — but with one twist. The first Messiah, son of Yosef, represents the reappearance of mercy. The ultimate Messiah, son of Yehudah/David, represents redemption and the return of sovereignty.

This scenario is exactly the drama of Yosef and Yehudah. In the struggle for royalty, Yosef appears to be the sovereign first. But he becomes the provider, showering necessities on his family; he dispenses mercy. Yet he is followed by Yehudah, who inherits royalty and brings ultimate redemption to Israel.

1. Ramban, Gen. 49:10.
2. Gen. 37:3.
3. Ibid. 37:13.

4. Ibid. 32:29, 35:10.
5. Ibid. 37:2.
6. Ibid. 37:3.
7. Ibid. 47:28.
8. Ibid. 47:29.
9. Ibid. 48:2.
10. Ibid. 48:3.
11. *Gen. Rabbah* 93.
12. Ramban, Deut. 31:18.
13. Deut. 31:16-18.

ספר שמות
Sefer Shemoth
The Book of Exodus

פרשת שמות
Parashath Shemoth

The Leader's Trials

ויהי בדרך במלון ויפגשהו ה׳ ויבקש המיתו.
"IT CAME TO PASS ON THE WAY, AT THE LODGING PLACE, [THAT] GOD APPROACHED [MOSHE] AND SOUGHT TO KILL HIM."
(Exodus 4:24)

This incident is one of the strangest and most inexplicable in the Torah. At its root is one great question: Why does God strike out against Moshe now? The intensity of God's anger is equally incomprehensible. At least on the surface, Moshe has done nothing to warrant such a severe penalty.

According to the Talmud — as quoted by Rashi — Moshe is guilty of failing to circumcise his son Eliezer.[1] Yet Talmudic sources find Moshe's neglect quite understandable: He has a mission to return to Egypt, and it would be dangerous for the child to travel immediately following circumcision.[2] Given this explanation, the harshness of his punishment becomes even more difficult.

One must also bear in mind that, Halachically, there is no death penalty or *kareth* for failure to circumcise one's son. This fate awaits only an uncircumcised adult and only —- rules Rambam — after his death.[3]

Perhaps the definition of a basic principle in Judaism is involved here. There is Talmudic evidence that whenever a ritual is attacked or acquires special importance because of current conditions or historical considerations, that practice becomes a fundamental tenet for which one must give his life.[4] Considering the Israelites' circumstances and Moshe's historic mission, perhaps circumcision had become such a principle. His neglect may therefore have evoked God's severest response.

Nevertheless, this episode calls for a more careful analysis:

In verse 18, Moshe announces that he is returning to his brothers in Egypt to see whether they are still alive, whereupon Yithro wishes his son-in-law a safe journey. Why does Moshe hide the purpose of his return? Why doesn't he mention that God has commanded him to redeem the Israelites by pleading their case before Pharaoh?

Verse 19 seems out of place. God's order that Moshe return to Egypt should have preceded his announcement of his journey.

This verse also gives a strange reason for Moshe's trip. God tells him to return to Egypt because the individuals who would harm him there have died. Yet, if Moshe has a Divine mission to perform, this technicality should hardly be a consideration.

Furthermore, verse 20 has a peculiar construction. First it relates that Moshe took his wife and sons and started toward Egypt. Then, almost as an afterthought, it states that he took God's staff with him. Conscious of this strange order, Rashi simply observes that chronology need not be exact in the Torah.

In fact, the next verse presents the same difficulty. God suddenly begins to advise Moshe about his mission although it would seem that this final Divine directive should precede the journey.

The end of the story, the drama of the circumcision, is extremely odd. Besides the difficulty recorded above, note Tzipporah's strange reactions: She circumcises her son and then tells her husband, "You are a bridegroom of blood unto me."[5] And after Moshe has been snatched from the jaws of death, she says, "A bridegroom of blood for circumcision."[6] What does this all mean? Rashi offers the traditional interpretation. But perhaps by rereading the story, we can translate these apparently key phrases more simply and uncover their historic implications.

When carefully examining the vision at the burning bush, God's order to appear before Pharaoh and redeem the Israelites, and Moshe's arguments against the mission, one notes that the prophet protests to the very end. God's anger notwithstanding, Moshe never really accepts the role of redeemer. Indeed, he announces that he is going to Egypt only to visit his brothers and inquire about their welfare. As a matter of fact, when he takes leave of Yithro, this is all Moshe intends to do.

God then instructs him not merely to visit Egypt but to live with his brothers again. For Moshe has always considered himself a stranger in Midian — hence the name of his son Gershom[7] — and felt that he must live and suffer with his brethren. He left the palace of Pharaoh, where he had grown up, just to be with them. Similarly, God tells him, he must leave the palace of Yithro and return to his brothers. The only reason he has left Egypt is that he is "wanted" there. God therefore informs him that the men who seek his death no longer exist, so he need not remain in Midian.

When Moshe intended simply to visit Egypt, he planned to travel alone. Now that he is to live there, however, he takes his wife and children. Almost as an afterthought, he also takes the "staff of God" with him, the staff which will serve as a symbol of leadership and Divine mission and as an instrument of miracles. This act is the first indication that Moshe may yet accept the task of redeeming Israel.

Verse follows verse so beautifully: Noting that Moshe takes the "staff of God" with him despite his vacillation, God dramatically spells out his mission and urges him to pursue it to its triumphant conclusion.

During their journey, Moshe and his family stop at an inn, possibly both to rest and to circumcise Eliezer. God then seeks to kill Moshe.

Perhaps this cryptic verse, couched in somewhat poetic or theological language, signifies that Moshe's tensions threaten his very life. On one hand, he fears himself incapable of such responsibility, and on the other, God insists that he accept it. On one hand, his humility and lack of self-confidence tell him to reject the offer; on the other, his concern for his brothers and their suffering weigh so heavily upon him. On one hand, he sincerely feels that someone else could do the job better; on the other, God commands: "Go to Pharaoh."

During his stay at the inn, amidst the respite from the hardships of his journey, Moshe reflects upon the tensions tearing him apart, upon his obligations and fears. His thoughts become so deep and intense that they threaten his life. God appears to him again, but his resistance to his mission is still so strong that he falls deathly ill.

Here, Tzipporah says and does something so dramatic that it decides the issue and directs the process of redemption and, to some extent, the entire course of Jewish history.

Moshe's wife declares, "...you are a bridegroom of blood unto me." This remark has little to do with Eliezer's circumcision, for that event just happens to coincide with our story. Rather, in effect, Tzipporah is saying to her husband: "When I consented to be your wife, you told me the history of your family and your people. You spoke of God's covenant with Avraham and the glorious future of your nation. You also explained the suffering your people must endure until its redemption. You underscored both the tragic and the heroic in your nation's past and future. I could have refused to marry you, choosing instead to remain in the sheltered palace of my father. I could have married within my people and enjoyed the luxuries of a princess. But I came with you and cast my lot with your people, realizing full well the difficulties I would face as part of this nation of God." And she takes the symbol of circumcision, the sign of the covenant, and places it at Moshe's feet, as though to tell him, "This is the covenant, and you must play your role in this historic drama."

Moshe then makes his decision. The pain and tension of his inner struggle subside, whereupon Tzipporah announces triumphantly, "A bridegroom of blood for circumcision," meaning, "My bridegroom, who is part of this great, eternal covenant, will now redeem the community of Israel, that it may fulfill its historic mission."

1. Rashi, Exod. 4:24; *Nedarim* 31b.
2. *Nedarim* 31b.
3. *Mishneh Torah*, "*Hilchoth Milah*" 1:1-2.
4. *Sanhedrin* 74b.
5. Exod. 4:25 and Rashi ad loc.
6. Exod. 4:26.
7. Exod. 2:22.

פרשת וארא
Parashath VaEira

The Naming

וארא אל אברהם אל יצחק ואל יעקב בקל שקי ושמי ה׳ לא נודעתי להם.
"I APPEARED UNTO AVRAHAM, UNTO YITZCHAK, AND UNTO YAAKOV WITH KEL SHADDAI — AND MY NAME HASHEM I DID NOT MAKE KNOWN TO THEM." (Exodus 6:3)

God's names figure prominently in this verse and its context. Rashi interprets these names as distinguishing between the posture of God who made promises to the patriarchs but could not yet keep His word and the posture of God now, when He comes to fulfill those promises. Entering into a highly mystical discussion of the names of God and their implications, Ramban quotes Ibn Ezra to the effect that Kel Shaddai betokens God who performed hidden miracles for the patriarchs without suspending natural law. In contradistinction, Hashem denotes God who transcends nature and alters its laws when necessary, e.g., in the redemption from Egypt, which entailed the suspension of natural law.[1]

Despite all these profound interpretations, there remains room for a simple translation of the text. Our analysis requires two introductory observations:

First, God appeared to the patriarchs as Kel Shaddai only when He changed Avraham's name and revealed to him the covenant of circumcision[2] and when Yaakov's name was changed, and His promises were repeated to him.³ (Yitzchak's essence is shrouded in mystery, and Kel Shaddai never appears in his prophecies.)

Second, commenting on the phrase "I appeared unto Avraham, unto Yitzchak, and unto Yaakov," Rashi remarks, "To the fathers."⁴ Commentaries have been hard put to explain this observation,⁵ for it seems to add nothing to our understanding of the text.

Let us now approach the verse from the following perspective: The patriarchs' encounters with God apparently play an important role here and must be seen on two levels. One, the patriarchs found and became associated with God and, through certain avenues (to be noted later), learned to know and understand Him. Two, God identified Himself to each patriarch in order to establish an eternal bond with him, which made him an *av*, a father.

In short, each patriarch must have become an *av* at a particular moment. This encounter with God was always with Kel Shaddai. Thus, when Avram was renamed Avraham, he became an *av*, and at that meeting God appeared as Kel Shaddai. And when Yaakov received the name Yisrael, he became an *av*, and then, too, God appeared as Kel Shaddai. As for Yitzchak, when God told him, "do not fear, for I am with you,"⁶ a promotion to the status of *av* was implied. Though the name Kel Shaddai is not mentioned, classic commentaries detect a reference to this name, however remote, in this case as well.

Yet this revelation, which establishes an *av*, must not be confused with the channel by which the patriarchs discovered God. Avraham found God through philosophy and abstract speculation, as described in Midrashic literature⁷ and in the first chapter of "Laws of Idolatry" in Rambam's *Mishneh Torah*. Yitzchak probably realized God in his first encounter with Him, the shattering experience of the *akeidah*, which presumably affected his religious and philosophic thought for the rest of his days. Yaakov found God in his dream of the ladder, which revealed his family history.

In short, Avraham found God through both nature and speculation, Yitzchak through the intensity of personal experience, and Yaakov through the intimate study of the history of Israel. But when they became *avoth*, the name Kel Shaddai figured supreme. Why?

In its simplest sense, *av* means "father." A father's relationship with his offspring is primarily physical. He endows his son with certain physical traits and psychological characteristics. Furthermore, by training his children, a father can develop and direct these traits and characteristics. In many senses, he should control his son's physical structure. The name Kel Shaddai implies, as indicated by Ibn Ezra and quoted in Ramban, that God controls the laws of nature which He created and by which He can perform hidden miracles. When Avraham, Yitzchak, and Yaakov became *avoth*, the "fathers" of their people, God therefore revealed Himself as Kel Shaddai.

How significant now is Rashi's observation that God appeared "to the fathers." For He appointed them patriarchs in a revelation of Kel Shaddai, stressing each one's particular relationship with God.

We can now examine Moshe's situation. When God revealed Himself to the prophet and directed him to approach the Israelites with the message of redemption, he asked which of His names he should use. The Divine reply, "*Ehyeh*,"[8] has been interpreted variously as the God who can be discovered through philosophic speculation,[9] profound personal experiences, or Jewish history,[10] as demonstrated by Avraham, Yitzchak, and Yaakov, respectively. But this relates only to finding God and recognizing His existence and truth.

Our text is quite revealing when we consider that perhaps here Moshe became not an *av* but the master of all prophets. Indeed, Moshe's mission was to become the prophet *par excellence*, receiving the Torah and transmitting it to Israel. The purpose of the Divine revelation in question, then, was to raise Moshe's stature. God was thus saying to him, "I, *Hashem*, hereby appoint you master of all prophets. For just as the Torah, which you are to receive, transcends nature and its laws, the name by which I associate Myself with you in this mission, Hashem, transcends reality. With Avraham, Yitzchak, and Yaakov, I was Kel Shaddai, because they were appointed *avoth*. But you have a different task, which I shall proceed to outline and which will lead to the dramatic climax of the revelation of the Torah at Sinai. Therefore, I appear to you as Hashem."

Additionally, the word *noda*, generally translated as "made known," as in our verse, "*lo nodati* — I did not make known," may imply intimate association. For the Torah says, "And the man *yada* his wife, Chavah...,"[11] which certainly refers to close connection. So, too, we may read this notion into the phrase used in our text — the position of *av* is intimately associated not with Hashem but with Kel Shaddai.

We may suggest an interesting and even exciting postscript to this discussion: Moshe became the master prophet right after attacking God's treatment of the suffering Israelites. No sooner did Moshe demonstrate his deep love for Israelites — to the point of disputing God — than he became worthy of the title "master of all prophets."

1. Ramban, Exod. 6:2.
2. Gen. 17:1.
3. Ibid. 35:11.
4. Rashi, Exod. 6:3.
5. Note *Sifthei Chachamim* ad loc.
6. Gen. 26:24.
7. *Gen. Rabbah* 39.

8. Exod. 3:14.
9. *Moreh Nevuchim*, pt. I, chs. 61-62.
10. Rashi, Exod. 3:14.
11. Gen. 4:1.
12. Exod. 5:22-23.

פרשת בא
Parashath Bo

Night of Watching

ליל שמרים הוא לה׳ להוציאם מארץ מצרים הוא הלילה הזה לה׳ שמרים לכל בני ישראל לדרתם.

"IT IS A NIGHT OF WATCHING UNTO GOD, TO TAKE THEM OUT OF THE LAND OF EGYPT; THIS IS THE NIGHT UNTO GOD, WATCHING FOR ALL THE CHILDREN OF ISRAEL THROUGHOUT THEIR GENERATIONS." (Exodus 12:42)

That this text is strange goes without saying. Its construction is complex and repetitive, its meaning vague and elusive.

Rashi interprets "night of watching" as the night for which God waited and watched in order to fulfill His promise of redemption. The expression "this is the night unto God" refers to the fact that this night had been anticipated since the covenant with Avraham. And "watching for all the children of Israel throughout their generations" implies that no harm can ever befall the children of Israel on this night.[1]

Ramban, however, writes that this night, which God anticipated for the purpose of redemption, is sanctified unto Him. For the children of Israel, too, it remains a night dedicated to God's praise and service.[2] What Ramban means by the night being sanctified unto God is unclear, but his interpretation does give the verse a certain unity.

Sforno echoes Rashi but adds that a night of "watching for all the children of Israel throughout their generations" refers to the anticipation of the ultimate redemption.[3] Somehow, according to Sforno, these words further suggest the notion that the exodus from Egypt was merely the beginning of a redemptive process that will be fully realized only in the final redemption.

Rashbam explains the phrase "watching for all the children of Israel" as implying the Jews' anticipation of this night each year in order to celebrate their redemption, perform the relevant commandments, and praise God.[4] Interestingly, this interpretation seems to explain the traditional preparation for Pesach which far exceeds the anticipation of other holidays. Aside from the required preparations, anticipating, or watching for, this night is apparently part and parcel of the celebration itself and inherent in Israel's consciousness.

I should now like to approach the text from a fresh perspective, prefacing my explanation with two observations:

First, the verse is out of place. It should have been recorded either along with the commandments, ceremonies, and laws of Pesach or in the drama of the redemption.

Second, the preceding verse reads, "...on this selfsame day, all the hosts of God went out of the land of Egypt."[5] The expression "*be'etzem hayom hazeh* — this selfsame day" is found several times in the Torah. This phrase generally indicates that the event it accompanies took place in daylight, i.e., in public view.[6] Here, too, it means that the Israelites left Egypt during the day. Now, such a statement followed by an ode to the preceding night of redemption requires some explanation.

Careful study of the two verses preceding our text will open a new avenue of analysis, which may lead to a very simple translation. These contradictory verses — 40 and 41 — present an interesting problem of timing. Verse 40 informs us that the children of Israel spent 430 years in Egypt, a figure not easily accounted for. Rashi and Ramban disagree regarding the beginning of this period.[7] According to Rashi, it commences with the Divine covenant with Avraham, which was finalized on the night of the fifteenth of Nissan. In the Torah, a day ends with either sunset or the onset of darkness that night. Thus, the 430 years concluded at nightfall on the fourteenth of Nissan.[8] Therefore, the exodus from Egypt should have occurred on the night of the fifteenth.

Verse 41, as noted, tells us that the Israelites did in fact leave Egypt on the fifteenth of Nissan — during the day. Consequently, we must account for the night of the fifteenth when they were still in Egypt.

I submit that verse 42, upon which we are focusing, solves this problem created by the two previous verses.

The drama of the exodus represents a complete suspension of the laws of nature,[9] affirming that the Creator can suspend whatever laws He put into operation. The *Meshech Chochmah*, explaining why the exodus took place at the beginning of the spring, develops very beautifully the notion that this season demonstrates the vitality of natural laws. After a long winter, the dormant powers of nature regenerate by blossoming in all their magnificent glory. God ordained, then, that precisely at this time should nature's laws be suspended and His will alone prevail. When the Haggadah states that, on the eve of the exodus, God operated without any other agents, it clearly means that all the laws of nature gave way to the will of God.

Therefore, though the Israelites were still in Egypt on the night of the fifteenth, that does not interfere with the exact count of 430 years. For this night transcends time. Since natural law was suspended in favor of God's will, the night is excluded from the usual reckoning of time. It belongs to God.

Let us now approach the problem on another level. Freedom need not relate to the physical exodus. Needless to say, its purpose was to bring the Israelites first to Mount Sinai to receive the Torah and eventually into their own land to build their own free and sovereign society. However, freedom begins when its anticipation is so real that it can already be celebrated as the fulfillment of God's will. Indeed, even while the Israelites were still in Egypt that night, by partaking of the Pesach sacrifice and reciting hymns of praise to God in spiritual exaltation, they became, in effect, a free people. Their anticipation that night was more than a dream; it was reality.[10]

Our verse is now so clear and simple. This is a night of watching, of realistic anticipation, and it is also a night that belongs to God. The text then explains each phrase. First, the night belonged to God and therefore transcended time. Second, it was a night of anticipated freedom for the Israelites, so even their presence in Egypt no longer constituted bondage.

1. Rashi, Exod. 12:42. Hence our abbreviated recitation of Shema on this night.
2. Ramban, Exod. 12:40.
3. Sforno, Exod. 12:42.
4. Rashbam, Exod. 12:42.
5. Exod. 12:41.
6. Note Gen. 7:13 and Rashi.
7. Rashi and Ramban, Exod. 12:40.
8. Cf. Sforno on Exod. 12:42, who suggests that from the exodus to the Messiah is one epic.
9. See *parashath VaEira*, "The Naming," where we have indicated that this suspension is the deeper meaning of the name "Hashem" which dominated that episode.
10. See *Berachoth* 4b and 9a regarding whether the exodus took place in the evening, too.

פרשת בשלח
Parashath BeShallach

Murmurings

וילונו כל עדת בני ישראל על משה ועל אהרן במדבר.
"THE WHOLE CONGREGATION OF THE CHILDREN OF ISRAEL MURMURED AGAINST MOSHE AND AHARON IN THE WILDERNESS." (Exodus 16:2)

The episode of the murmurers is unusually complex, with textual and logical difficulties abounding from beginning to end. Let us outline the obvious difficulties step by step and verse by verse.

The Israelites complain, and God's response is immediate. In verse 4, God tells Moshe that He is prepared to give them *lechem*, bread, from the heavens. Yet, in verse 12, God informs Moshe that He has heard the complaints of the Israelites, and that they will receive meat and bread. How can one reconcile these two Divine statements?

Additionally, in God's first pronouncement (verses 4-5), He says that the Israelites will receive bread, or food, each day and a double portion on Friday. Why mention Shabbath now?

Moshe's reaction is equally strange. In verses 6-7, he and Aharon inform the Israelites that "in the evening, you will know that God took you out of the land of Egypt. And in the morning, you will see the glory of God...." Oddly enough, there is no reference here to meat and bread, while in verse 8, Moshe seems to respond to just such a request, which he says will be fulfilled. However, Moshe has received no directive from God to speak about meat. This problem might revolve around whether the word "*lechem*" means "bread" or "food." The Torah quotes God as speaking of bread, but perhaps Moshe's prophecy included meat as well. Still, it is all extremely confusing.

Furthermore, though verses 6-7 quote Moshe and Aharon, verse 8 — which speaks of bread and meat — is attributed to Moshe alone. And in verse 9, surprisingly, Moshe directs Aharon to tell the people that God has heard their complaint.

A careful reading of the Israelites' complaint reveals its ambiguity. They simply lament that it would have been better to die by God's hand in Egypt than to starve to death in the wilderness. Elsewhere, the children of Israel state clearly that they need water, they are tired of simple, bland food, or they want meat. Here, however, they merely allude to the meat and bread they enjoyed in Egypt and refer more specifically to their fate and future.

I submit, therefore, that their complaint is both an ideological question or grievance and an expression of their desire for the luxuries to which they grew accustomed in Egypt. Our passage treats this complaint on both levels.

Ideologically, the Israelites case is strong. The exodus seems senseless if they are to die of hunger in the wilderness. This argument resembles Avraham's, as recorded in the Midrash, concerning the binding of Yitzchak. Avraham maintains that he cannot understand the ways of God. Yesterday, he was told that his seed will issue from Yitzchak, while today Avraham is told to sacrifice his son.[1] So, too, the Israelites contend: Yesterday, we were miraculously redeemed from Egypt, and today we will starve to death. What, then, is the point of this game?

God's response now becomes clear. In verses 4-5, He indicates the purpose of the drama as far as the Jews are concerned: to affirm God's existence, omnipotence, and concern for His people. No miracle so dramatized God's will and Israel's reliance upon Him as did the manna from heaven. In the middle of a dark and desolate wilderness with no food or water, they receive from the heavens one day's worth of food. Can one begin to imagine the faith of the individual who goes to sleep at night without a morsel of food in his house for himself or his children? He must feel with overpowering conviction that his household's sustenance will materialize in the morning, and, even then, he can only pray that it is there. But this precarious position serves only to strengthen his faith in the existence and beneficence of God.

Moreover, the fact that there will be no manna on Shabbath and a double portion on Friday further corroborates the truth of Creation. Thus, through manna, the very objective of the exodus will be achieved. God's existence, His role as Creator, and His sustenance of human life will all be emphasized.

Thus, in verses 6-7, Moshe and Aharon interpret the essence of God's first message to the Israelites. In the evening, when they go to sleep praying for food and filled with faith in God, they will recognize the purpose of the exodus. In the morning, when they find their prayers answered and their faith strengthened, they will see the glory of God in all its complete brilliance, continuing the Divine intervention that made the exodus possible. So much for the Israelites' idelological arguments.

Beneath the ideology, however, one detects an almost selfish nostalgia for the bread and meat of Egypt. The very fact that they mention these foods reveals the inconceivable lust underneath all the fine philosophy.

Interestingly, Aharon barely notices or reacts to this desire. Never questioning people's motives, peaceloving Aharon,[2] cannot conceive of the forces underlying the Israelites sophisticated ideological arguments.

But Moshe can. Therefore, in verse 8, Moshe himself tells

the people that beneath their philosophizing, he recognizes their base desire for meat, which God will satisfy.

We now note the tension between Moshe and Aharon. Suddenly, Moshe bids his brother to tell the people to come forth, for God has heard their complaint. Aharon is to inform them that not only will God respond to their argument regarding the purpose of the exodus, but He will satisfy their craving.

We now understand Moshe's differing reaction in verses 7 and 8. In the former, he utters the famous words "What are we, that you complain against us?" In the latter, though he repeats this expression, he emphasizes that the Israelites are complaining against God, and he implies that they will be punished for it. Additionally, the Midrash observes that, in verse 7, Moshe considers himself unable to reply, while in verse 8, Moshe responds angrily when the glory of God is at stake.[3]

In keeping with our analysis, the distinction is quite obvious. In the first case, addressing the ideological argument, Moshe stresses that he, too, cannot fathom God's ways but must rely upon Divine revelation. In the second case, replying to the less sophisticated cry for luxuries, he denounces the people's argument against God.

1. *Gen. Rabbah* 56:15.
2. *Avoth* 1:12.
3. *Mechilta, BeShallach* 4:2.

פרשת יתרו
Parashath Yithro

A Father's Role

וישמע יתרו כהן מדין חתן משה את כל אשר עשה אלקים למשה ולישראל עמו כי הוציא ה' את ישראל ממצרים.

"YITHRO, PRIEST OF MIDIAN, FATHER-IN-LAW OF MOSHE, HEARD ALL THAT GOD HAD DONE FOR MOSHE AND FOR HIS PEOPLE, ISRAEL, FOR GOD HAD BROUGHT ISRAEL OUT OF EGYPT." (Exodus 18:1)

Our text introduces the reunion between Moshe and his family, describing the events that induced Yithro to greet Moshe and bring Tzipporah and the children along. There are so many oddities here, though, that we would do well to take them step by step.

In a very famous comment, Rashi insists that what Yithro heard, and apparently what moved him, was the parting of the Red Sea and the battle with Amalek.[1] However, "all that God had done" refers to "the manna, the well [of water], and Amalek."[2] The problem is clear: Rashi should have stated at the outset that all these phenomena inspired Yithro, or should have included everything in his second comment. Additionally, why does he repeat Amalek?

Furthermore, this verse relates "Yithro...heard all that *Elokim* had done for Moshe...for *Hashem* had brought Israel out of Egypt." How can one explain this discrepancy? The very specific implications of God's names must be understood within this context.

Subsequent verses tell us that Yithro took Tzipporah and her two children to Moshe.[3] Surprisingly, the text provides not only the children's names but their derivation.[4] While one may build a case as Ramban does, for recording Eliezer's name and its source — which have not yet appeared in the Torah — why are Gershom's name and derivation repeated when both are given at his birth?[5]

Moshe's interpretation of the name Eliezer is also rather remarkable: "...for the God of my father was my help, and He saved me from Pharaoh's sword." *Eli* means "my God," not "the God of my father." How, then, does the name allude to the latter?

Returning to our first question, I think Rashi does not repeat himself regarding Amalek; he speaks of different things. First, commenting on "Yithro heard," Rashi explains that Moshe's father-in-law heard about the miracle of the splitting of the Red Sea and the war with Amalek. Then, focusing on "all that God had done," Rashi cites "the manna, the well, and Amalek." Apparently Rashi emphasizes first the war, then the victory.

Significantly, Yithro appears here as both a religious personage and Moshe's father-in-law. His reactions stemmed from both identities.

As a Midianite priest, Yithro was deeply concerned with this new religious phenomenon. As he later says, he recognized a fresh dimension of religious experience through the recent history of the Jewish people, a people that bore God's name, and consequently enraged His enemies. When foxes attacked the Temple mount, as the Talmud beautifully relates, Rabbi Akiva laughed.[6] To him, the sacrilege reflected the sanctity of the mount which attracted even foxes. Likewise, Yithro was drawn to Israel when he saw that, even after the miracles at the Red Sea, Amalek still hounded this people. To Yithro, this act of war indicated the importance of the Jews and their message. In his religious capacity, therefore, he had

A Father's Role

to meet and try to understand this nation. Hence, Rashi's first comment: Yithro came to Moshe because of two successive events — the miracle at the Red Sea and the war with Amalek. This priest of Midian reacts to a major religious phenomenon.

But there is much more — and here the story becomes particularly fascinating and the text remarkably clear.

In His mercy, God redeemed the Israelites. As a result — as Ramban stresses repeatedly — the Israelites belong to God. He acquired them.[7] Accordingly, justice dictated that He provide them with the basic necessities of food, water, and shelter, i.e., protection from elements and enemies. And indeed, He did. Yithro saw that Elokim, God of justice, granted the Israelites food, water, and victory over Amalek, because Hashem, God of compassion, had liberated them from Egyptian bondage. Freeing the Jewish people imposed obligations upon God, and He fulfilled them.

This brings us to the principle of *imitatio Dei*, the emulation of God. If a father brings life into the world, then he is responsible for this child. Just as God provided for the Israelites after giving them a new life, a father must provide for his offspring. Thus, Moshe's father-in-law brought Tzipporah and her children to their husband and father, for a parent must care for his children.

We have demonstrated how Yithro was moved both religiously and personally. However, another consideration penetrates this episode even more deeply. Perhaps Yithro recognized that his grandchildren's spiritual development required involvement with their people and the guidance of their father. If so, Yithro took his cue from Moshe himself.

Moshe lived with his father-in-law in comparative peace and probable comfort. But Moshe named one of his sons Gershom, for he still considered himself a stranger in a strange land. His heart magnetically drew him to his suffering brethren in Egypt. He belonged with them, sharing their fate. And indeed, only after Moshe gave his son this name did God reveal the prophet's redemptive mission.[8]

Moreover, God introduced Himself to Moshe as the God of his father. The Midrash even dramatically suggests that God's voice resembled Amram's, such that Moshe thought his father was calling him.[9] For no religious experience begins in a vacuum; it develops over generations and is transmitted from father to son.

Hence the mention of Moshe's children by name here. Yithro was virtually saying to Moshe, "You named your son Gershom because you were a stranger in Midian, isolated from your people. Your sons, too, must live with their people and share its history. You named your son Eliezer, but you did not say, '*My* God was my help'; rather, you invoked 'for the God *of my father.*' And you were right. One experiences God through his father. So how can you deprive your children of these two pivotal experiences, being part of their people and receiving their father's tradition?"

Bearing all this in mind, Yithro brought Tzipporah and her children to Moshe, reminding him of his paternal responsibilities both physically and spiritually. Most important, Moshe was reminded to strive for *imitatio Dei*.

1. Rashi, Exod. 18:1.
2. Ibid.
3. Exod. 18:2-3.
4. Ibid. 18:3-4.
5. Ibid. 2:22.
6. *Makkoth* 24b.
7. Ramban, Exod. 6:6.
8. Exod. 3:1.
9. *Exod. Rabbah* 3:1.

פרשת משפטים
Parashath Mishpatim

HUMAN FREEDOM

ואלה המשפטים אשר תשים לפניהם. כי תקנה עבד עברי שש שנים יעבד ובשבעת יצא לחפשי חנם.

"AND THESE ARE THE LAWS THAT YOU SHALL SET BEFORE THEM: IF YOU BUY A HEBREW SERVANT, SIX YEARS HE SHALL WORK, AND IN THE SEVENTH HE SHALL GO FREE."

(Exodus 21:1-2)

Verses dealing with laws must be interpreted in Halachic terms. Indeed, both the Midrash and the Talmud dwell upon and interpret every word and letter in *Parashath Mishpatim*. However, all this scrutiny should not deter us from exploring the motifs underlying these laws.

Interestingly, the Torah begins its legal code with the laws of slavery. An overview of this phenomenon will pave the way for our point here.

To meet with God and receive His Torah, the Israelites had to satisfy two conditions. Before the revelation, "Israel camped there by the mountain."[1] Our rabbis point out that the verb "camped" is singular,[2] implying that national unity was necessary for receiving the Torah. Furthermore, when Moshe outlined for the Israelites' preparations for this event, his major directive was, "do not come near a woman,"[3] i.e., purity in intimate relations was another prerequisite.

It is extremely significant that, following the revelation, the Israelites are told that whenever they call on God via an earthen altar and sacrifices, He will appear and bless them.[4] This juxtaposition stresses that revelation can recur anytime albeit perhaps in another form. But again, there are two conditions, which are presented somewhat symbolically. The text tells us that a stone altar must not be subjected to the sword.[5] The Torah also states that there must not be steps leading to the altar, for climbing stairs in priestly garb would be immodest.[6] Scripture, then, is reemphasizing the two prerequisites of revelation: unity — hence the prohibition of lethal weapons; and purity — hence the prohibition of anything inviting to immorality.

The first two institutions described in our *parashah* actually refer to and clarify these motifs:

The laws of the Hebrew servant as expressed here stress freedom. The subjugation of one human being by another is akin to use of the sword and therefore discourages revelation. Practically every *pasuk* begins with a condition and concludes with a form of emancipation, as though emphasizing that the very purpose of the institution of a Hebrew servant is to free him.[7]

In contrast, regarding the Hebrew maidservant, emancipation is practically ruled out in the very first verse.[8] For this institution is to bring about marriage between maid and master. A penniless girl with no marital prospects presents a serious problem that may lead to promiscuity. Servitude, therefore, is intended to offer her a full, pure, and meaningful life.

These observations indicate continuity between the revelation and the Torah institutions here, as expressed by the conjunction "*And* these are the laws...," a phrase that has inspired many interpretations.[9]

Returning to the institution of the Hebrew servant and its underlying principle — man should be free of all servitude — let us concentrate upon one word crucial to the whole passage: *begapo,* a difficult word to translate.

The third verse of our portion reads, "If he enters *begapo*, he must leave *begapo*, if he has a wife, his wife must leave with him." Verse 4 reads, "If his master gives him a wife, and she bears him sons or daughters, the wife and her children shall be her master's, and he shall go out *begapo*." (We should point out that the wife given to him by his master is a Canaanite maidservant, and therefore exempt from the laws of a Hebrew maid.)

Rashi interprets *begapo* to mean that the servant came in his coat,[10] i.e., he entered his master's service alone, without a wife. Ibn Ezra likewise takes *begapo* as *begufo*, by himself.[11] According to both explanations, *begapo* is negative, but this expression is always positive. Here, too, the servant came *with* something — something called *gapo*. What is it? How and why must it be retained?

This Jew entered into servitude with *gapo* — himself, his dignity, his self-esteem. Though economics forced him into slavery, he has not forfeited his honor, his self-respect, or his pride. And the Torah insists that when he rejoins the free world and reclaims his position in society, he should do so *begapo*, with his respectability and self-worth intact.

Moreover, a master cares for the physical needs of his Hebrew servant's Jewish wife. When this servant is freed, however, the Torah demands that his wife leave with him and that he provide for her — two signs of his dignity and self-respect. On the other hand, when a non-Hebrew wife is given to him as part of his servitude, she and her children stay behind when he regains his freedom, for by remaining attached to her and their children, he would retain a constant mark of enslavement and lose that precious *gapo*.

However, there is a serious problem here. This Hebrew servant has fathered a non-Hebrew maid's children, even if Halachically one can argue that they are not his. It may seem cruel to require that he abandon them. But apparently the Torah feels that this course is best for all concerned, and we must accept it. We must not engage in apologetics.

Yet this law applies only to a Jew who enters into servitude *begapo*. Without this ingredient, there is no point in severing these relations. If a servant states that he loves his master, his non-Hebrew wife, and his children and would rather not leave them, he has clearly lost *gapo*, or perhaps he never had it. Consequently, he remains enslaved forever.[12]

But *our* goal is freedom, the message of the exodus.

1. Exod. 19:2.
2. Note Rashi and *Mechilta*, Exod. 19:2.
3. Ibid. 19:15.
4. Ibid. 20:21.
5. Ibid. 20:22.
6. Ibid 20:23.
7. Ibid. 21:1-6.
8. Ibid. 21:7-11.
9. Note Rashi, *Or HaChayim*, and *Mechilta*, Exod. 21:1.
10. Rashi, Exod. 21:3.
11. Ibn Ezra, Exod. 21:3.
12. Exod. 21:5-6.

פרשת תרומה
Parashath Terumah

Holiness and Separation

דבר אל בני ישראל ויקחו לי תרומה מאת כל איש אשר ידבנו לבו תקחו את תרומתי.

"SPEAK UNTO THE CHILDREN OF ISRAEL, AND THEY SHALL TAKE UNTO ME A *TERUMAH*; FROM EVERY MAN WHOSE HEART SHALL OFFER A CONTRIBUTION, YOU SHALL TAKE MY *TERUMAH*." (Exodus 25:2)

This verse introduces the Divine directive to collect from the Israelites various materials with which to build a sanctuary. The textual problems here are many, and some are quite intricate, but we shall mention only those that concern our theme.

All the commentaries note that "and they shall take" should really read, "and they shall give."[1]

Furthermore, though verses 3-7 list the materials to be used for building the sanctuary, we would certainly not expect the Torah to specify their purposes before the actual construction directive in the verses. Thus, the intent of the gold, silver, copper, and skins is not yet revealed. Why, then, does the Torah immediately divulge that oil is for lighting, incense for anointing, spices for anointing oil and incense, and precious stones for the high priest's vest and breastplate.[2] These functions are spelled out before we know anything about a sanctuary. Additional information may have been related orally to Moshe, lending these phrases a context, but the text should have its own dimensions.

There is a fascinating discussion among the commentators regarding the command to build the sanctuary. The Torah states: "They shall make a sanctuary for Me; I shall dwell among them. According to all that I show you, the form of the tabernacle and the form of all its vessels, and shall you do."[3] This last phrase, "and so shall you do," seems redundant. Rashi therefore suggests that, while the first directive, "They shall make a sanctuary for Me," refers to the generation in the wilderness, the second phrase addresses future generations.[4]

Ramban questions Rashi's interpretation,[5] but its biggest difficulty is grammatical. While verse 8 is in third person — "They shall make...," verse 9 is in second person — "...so shall you do." Both phrases should be in either second or third person. And according to Rashi, the command intended for the current generation is in third person, while the clause directed at future generations is in second person. This strange construction should have been reversed.

To appreciate this magnificent Torah discussion, one must consider two fundamental principles:

First, *kedushah*, holiness, is intimately related to *havdalah*, separation. Holiness is the readiness to separate element from element, area from area, experience from experience. Thus, wherever the Torah commands us to be holy, it also insists upon *havdalah*.[6]

Therefore, when Rashi translates *mikdash* as *beith k'dushah*,[7] a house of holiness, his implication is that every form of holiness, and consequently every form of separation, is embodied in this institution. The sanctuary expresses and, if you wish, symbolizes, the various areas of *k'dushah* or *havdalah*. This is its basic and essential nature and everything else in it is peripheral.

Our passage is not intended to convey the uses of the materials to be donated; their functions become clear when the various vessels are discussed and their construction described in the minutest detail. Rather, the Torah is defining the nature of the sanctuary, *the* repository of holiness, by singling out articles and materials that illustrate some category of *havdalah*.

Our Havdalah ceremony notes four main separations: sacred versus secular, light versus darkness, Israel versus the nations, and "holy versus holy," i.e., Shabbath versus festivals. Likewise, the oil that lights the lamp illuminates the *havdalah* between light and darkness. The stones of the vest and breastplate, upon which the tribes of Israel were inscribed, separate Israel from the nations. The vessels Moshe constructs are consecrated through anointment (whereas, in later history, their use in the Temple sanctified them). Thus, the anointing oil differentiates between sacred and secular. And the incense addresses itself to the soul, signifying the subtle distinctions between holy and holy.

These materials are set apart — by the enunciation of their purpose — because they express the essence of the *mikdash*, the *beith kedushah*. They typify the differentiations at the heart of the sanctuary.

As for the second principle, it may appear homiletical, but it is founded on Halachah:

Offering *terumah*, a priestly gift, involves two stages: *hafrashah* (separation) and *nethinah* (giving). *Hafrashah* means separating part of one's produce and pronouncing it holy. The remaining produce then becomes fit for consumption. Following this separation, one must give the *terumah* to a *kohen* (priest).

Thus, the Torah demands that the Jew sanctify something while it is still his. Only then does he offer it to the *kohen*. For *kedushah* begins in the home before it becomes part of the general religious institution.

Our text is now quite clear. "They shall *take...terumah*" rather than give it, because before Moshe and his committee could accept donations for the sanctuary, the Israelites had to sanctify them by *hafrashah*.

In essence, two sanctuaries are being fashioned. While Moshe builds the Tabernacle, each Israelite makes his home a repository of *kedushah* and *havdalah* as well by performing *hafrashah* there. In fact, the construction and sanctity of the central *mikdash* are dependent upon and proportionate to the holiness of Israel's individual sanctuaries. After all, they are where Moshe gets his materials.

In verses 8-9, God tells Moshe in effect, "Let them — the Israelites — build a sanctuary of their homes, and I shall dwell among them. Meanwhile, you — Moshe — and your committee shall do likewise in building the central *mikdash*." Hence the shift from third person to second.

Thus, when the commentaries note that "I shall dwell among *them*" means among the Israelites, not in the central *mikdash*, it is not far-fetched homiletics — it is the simple translation.

1. See Sforno, *Or HaChayim* on Exod. 25:2.
2. Exod. 25:6, 7.
3. Ibid. 25:8-9.
4. Rashi, Exod. 25:9.
5. Ramban, Exod. 25:9.
6. Note Lev. 19:2.
7. Rashi, Exod. 25:8.

פרשת תצוה
Parashath Tetzaveh

Continuous Light

ואתה תצוה את בני ישראל ויקחו אליך שמן זית זך כתית למאור להעלת נר
תמיד. באהל מועד מחוץ לפרכת אשר על העדת יערך אתו אהרן ובניו מערב עד
בקר לפני ה' חקת עולם לדרתם מאת בני ישראל.

"AND YOU SHALL COMMAND THE CHILDREN OF ISRAEL, AND THEY SHALL TAKE UNTO YOU PURE OLIVE OIL, PRESSED, FOR LIGHTING, TO BRING FORTH LIGHT CONTINUOUSLY. IN THE *OHEL MO'ED*, OUTSIDE THE DIVIDING CURTAIN, WHICH IS OVER THE TESTIMONY, AHARON AND HIS CHILDREN SHALL TEND IT FROM EVENING TO MORNING BEFORE GOD [AS] AN EVERLASTING LAW FOR THEIR GENERATIONS FROM THE CHILDREN OF ISRAEL." (Exodus 27:20-21)

Let us enumerate the problems — some obvious, some not — in these two verses.

1. The second-person expression "and you shall command" is noteworthy since it is followed by a similar form, "And, draw Aharon near...."[1]

2. Classic commentators have wondered why the oil must be brought to Moshe. Ramban suggests that Moshe is to judge whether it is proper for the delicate purpose of lighting.[2] Rather pointedly, Netziv rejects this explanation, for what would happen after Moshe passes on?[3]

3. Why is the position of the menorah repeated here? It is already detailed in the section that deals with the menorah's construction amidst the other vessels of the sanctuary.[4]

Moreover, how is this law "...from the children of Israel"? Ramban claims that the oil shall be taken from whichever Israelites contribute it.[5] But this arrangement, too, has been stipulated previously.

4. Isn't every precept "an everlasting law for their generations"? Furthermore, this law applies only in the Temple period, not in exile.

5. The previous *parashah*, *Terumah*, is devoted almost exclusively to the sanctuary and its vessels. *Tetzaveh*, though, focuses on the functionaries of the sanctuary, Aharon and his sons, and their priestly attire. Accordingly, our passage, which speaks about oil and the menorah, seems out of place.

6. Even more peculiar, Aharon and his sons are commanded to kindle the menorah even before being singled out as functionaries of the sanctuary. Only immediately afterwards is Moshe told to draw Aharon and his sons near as priests.[6] It is a rather strange juxtaposition of information.

Another very relevant observation has been made by *Or HaChayim*,[7] which notes a remarkable parallelism between the opening verses of *Terumah* and *Tetzaveh*. Both feature the expression "they shall take." Furthermore, there we read, "...I shall dwell among them"; here we read, "...from the children of Israel." There it says, "Speak unto the children of Israel..."; here it states, "And you shall command the children of Israel...." The likeness is very subtle, yet one senses it in the rhythm of these two openings.

Our rabbis point out that in *Tetzaveh*, Moshe's name is omitted. Even classic commentators have reacted to this phenomenon,[8] indicating that it is no mere homiletic nicety and should be considered rather carefully.

I should like to approach the matter as both a problem and an essential principle of Jewish philosophy. The problem is Moshe himself, and the philosophic principle concerns his status.

It may come as a shock to Moshe that, after he has

engineered the redemption of the people from Egypt and dominated the drama of revelation, responsibility for the sanctuary and its service is handed over to Aharon and his children. Moshe's children are not even given any special status within the Temple. Therefore, if Aharon and sons are charged with lighting the menorah even before they are singled out as functionaries of the sanctuary, it may be in order to soften the blow and ease Moshe's pain. One need not assume jealousy on Moshe's part — that would hardly be in character — to posit that the Torah introduces Aharon and his children gradually.

However, these two verses go much farther: They define Moshe's dominion. It is as though the Torah were saying, "Aharon and his sons are to officiate in the sanctuary: They will wear the vestments in glory and holiness, they will offer sacrifices, and they will be the custodians of this sacred service, which mystically fuses God's glory with the congregation of Israel. But you, Moshe, will be the teacher, and your position transcends theirs."

Aharon might offer sacrifices, but Moshe informs him of how to do so. Aharon may function in the sanctuary, but Moshe elucidates its nature. Aharon wears the vestments; Moshe describes and designs them. In short, while Aharon *fulfills* God's will in the sanctuary, Moshe *transmits* it. Aharon may have priesthood, but Moshe has royalty — the royalty of the Torah and its teachers.

We are not particularly given to symbolism, and our analysis of the text stands on its own. Nonetheless, both the Midrash and our classic commentaries connect the light of the menorah and the light of the Torah.[9] The Torah's interjection regarding the lighting of the menorah, to be done under Moshe's direction and examination, has special significance. For Moshe is established here as the eternal teacher of Torah and the exclusive interpreter and transmitter of God's word and will.

THE DEPTHS OF SIMPLICITY

Let us now reread our text and note the points and principles we have emphasized.

Moshe commands the Israelites even as God does. He also examines the oil, for he represents the will of God. While the lighting of the menorah relates only to the Temple period, the more basic principle — namely, that Moshe transmits God's will — is always relevant. Perhaps then, "an everlasting law for their generations" refers not to the kindling of the menorah but to the phrase "and *you* shall command."

The menorah's position is described here for purposes of contrast. Aharon and his sons will light the menorah outside the curtain dividing the holy from the Holy of Holies. But Moshe functions inside the Holy of Holies. His commands come directly from the ark of testimony.

Furthermore — and most important — Aharon's task is limited to one family. Only he and his descendants can serve in the sanctuary. Moshe's purview, however, is not restricted to Moshe and his sons. The primacy of Torah and its teaching is so fundamental that no Jew is excluded; it is open to all. The expression "from the children of Israel" therfore suggests that the entire congregation of Israel can attain the crown of Torah.

Likewise, Moshe's name is missing from this *parashah* to emphasize that the royalty of Torah, instituted here, is available to all. The priesthood is dynastic, but the royalty of Torah is democratic; it has nothing to do with genealogy.

Anyone who studies, understands, knows, and commits himself to Torah becomes the interpreter of God's will in the royal chain of our oral tradition. To him as well as to Moshe, the expression "and you shall command" is directed.

1. Exod. 28:1.
2. Ramban, Exod. 27:20.
3. *Ha'amek Davar*, Exod. 27:20.
4. Exod. 40:24.
5. Ramban, Exod. 27:20.
6. Exod. 28:1.
7. *Or HaChayim*, Exod. 27:20.
8. Note *Baal HaTurim*, Exod. 27:20.
9. *Ha'amek Davar* and Malbim.

פרשת כי תשא
Parashath Ki Thissa

Seek the Miraculous

ויאמר משה אל ה' ראה אתה אמר אלי העל את העם הזה ואתה לא הודעתני את אשר תשלח עמי ואתה אמרת ידעתיך בשם וגם מצאת חן בעיני.

"AND MOSHE SAID TO GOD: 'SEE, YOU SAY UNTO ME, "BRING THIS PEOPLE UP," AND YOU HAVE NOT LET ME KNOW WHAT YOU WILL SEND WITH ME; AND YOU HAVE SAID, "I KNOW YOU BY NAME, AND YOU HAVE ALSO FOUND FAVOR IN MY EYES."'"

(Exodus 33:12)

This verse opens a highly mystical passage that resists translation. We shall note Rashi's interpretation,[1] make some observations, and then explain the text in its simplest form.

First, Rashi maintains, when Moshe states that he has not been told whom or what God will send with him, he is protesting His promise that an angel will lead the children of Israel into the land.[2] As is well known, there are different opinions regarding this agent, but Rashi stands by his theory. Moshe is, in effect, telling God that he wants Him, not an angel.

Second, when Moshe says, "You have said, 'I know you by name,'" this means, according to Rashi, that God granted him credibility through the drama of revelation at Sinai, and consequently the Israelites will forever accept his teachings.

Third, when, in the next verse, Moshe asks God to reveal His way,[3] he is simply inquiring about the reward accruing to someone who finds favor in His eyes. In fact, Moshe seeks his own reward. What, then, is the meaning of the concluding

112

Seek the Miraculous

phrase, "...and see that this people is Your nation"?[4] Rashi explains that Moshe is pleading with God to spare the people. But how does this plea follow from his previous request? Mizrachi suggests that Moshe wants to know what reward he will receive for leading God's nation.[5] However, it is more characteristic of Rashi to understand Moshe as saying that his greatest reward lies in this people remaining the *people of God. He seeks only that God lead his nation by His own glory.

God answers, "My presence will go; I will give you rest."[6] While there are many translations and interpretations of this verse, Rashi insists that God is granting Moshe's wish. And when he repeats, "If Your presence does not go, do not bring us up from here,"[7] he is merely emphasizing that God will indeed go with the people. God has retracted, so to speak, His intent to send an angel as His agent.

Such is Rashi's view, with which Ramban has great difficulty.[8]

I should like to pose three queries concerning the numerous interpretations of Moshe's request, "please let me know Your way," as an appeal to learn more about God's justice or mercy.

First, what prompts Moshe to make such a demand at this stage of the unfolding story of *b'nei Yisrael*? A request to know God would seem more appropriate when the people are in His good graces, not when they have just transgressed with the golden calf.

Second, where indeed has God said, "I know you by name"? Because there is no such statement in the text, Rashi interprets "by name" as refering not to God's name — the phrase's usual meaning — but to Moshe's, as indicated above. But Rashi's is not the simple translation of the verse.

Third, "...and see that this people is Your nation" still appears out of place. While Rashi's interpretation has its charm, it is not contextual. Ramban comments on this phrase,

113

"You are their Father, and they are Your children."⁹ What does this add to one's understanding of text and context?

One more observation: Verse 14, speaks of "My face," and verse 15 of "Your face." Ramban implies that the first expression refers to Divine justice, perhaps tempered by mercy, whereas the second term reflects the closest relationship between God and Israel.¹⁰ Again, what does this distinction mean to us?

As mentioned, these verses are steeped in mysticism and almost defy simple translation. However, certain considerations are so clear that we cannot help pointing them out and drawing the obvious conclusions.

When God met Moshe at the burning bush and instructed him to redeem the Jewish people, his mission was limited to pleading the Jews' case, impressing upon them the nature of their unfolding Divine redemption, leading them out of Egypt, and receiving the Torah at Mount Sinai.¹¹ There was no indication that Moshe was to lead the Jewish people into the promised land. On the contrary, his sole purpose would be to teach Torah, interpreting the word and will of God. This role explains why, immediately preceding our text, Moshe converts his tent into a meeting place for those seeking God.¹² Now that both exodus and revelation are completed, he fades into the background, retaining only his teaching position.

But just then, Moshe receives a new mission: to lead the Israelites into the land that was promised them. If we bear this new direction in mind, his request in verses 12-13 suddenly becomes meaningful, characteristic, and almost simple.

When Moshe was first directed to redeem the Israelites, he replied that they would ask the name of this God who had appeared to him. As Ramban writes, God's name indicates His form of revelation. Thus, the people would seek to ascertain with what Divine attributes or in what form their redemption would take place.¹³ Would it be through miracles or through strange interrelated routine events? God answered that He would appear as Hashem, implying that the redemption would be miraculous.

Here, then, newly commanded to lead the Israelites into the land, Moshe wants to know the same thing. But, very significantly, he refers to precedent. When he accepted his first mission, God made known to him which Divine name would dominate the drama of redemption. This is what Moshe means by God knowing him by name. Likewise, Moshe must know which attributes of God will propel the Jews into the land. Thus, when he asks God to reveal His ways, he is repeating a request made back when he was to redeem the Israelites.

Moreover, Moshe pleads that, despite the recent transgression of the golden calf, "...this people is Your nation" — "You are their Father, and they are Your children." Therefore, he urges, Divine mercy — accompanied by miracles — should predominate.

Finally, we must distinguish between two terms: "*yeileichu*" in verse 14 and "*holchim*" in verse 15. While both mean "go," the former connotes "going away," while the latter suggests "going with."

God assures Moshe that His anger (or attribute of justice) will slowly "go away" and be mitigated by mercy. Yet Moshe demands that God's complete compassion accompany the people. And, indeed, his request is granted, and the attributes of Divine mercy are dramatically revealed.[14]

The dialogue is now quite clear. It parallels the discussion between God and Moshe at the burning bush, for doubts and anxieties about the relationship between God and Israel assail the prophet whenever he undertakes a mission.

1. Rashi, Exod. 33:15.
2. Exod. 23:20.
3. Ibid. 33:13.

4. Ibid.
5. Note *Sifthei Chachamim,* Exod. 33, note 5.
6. Exod. 33:14.
7. Ibid. 33:15.
8. Ramban, Exod. 33:13.
9. Ibid., Exod. 33:14.
10. Ibid.
11. Exod. 3:1-12.
12. Ibid. 33:7-11.
13. Ramban, Exod. 3:13.
14. Exod. 34:6-7.

פרשת ויקהל
Parashath VaYakhel

FIRE AS A SYMBOL

לא תבערו אש בכל משבתיכם ביום השבת.
"YOU SHALL NOT KINDLE FIRE IN ALL YOUR HABITATIONS ON THE SHABBATH DAY." (Exodus 35:3)

Before informing *b'nei Yisrael* of the Divine commandment to build a sanctuary, Moshe outlines the fundamental laws of Shabbath. He emphasizes that work is prohibited on Shabbath and that any transgression of this law carries the death penalty.[1] The relationship between the construction of the sanctuary and the observance of Shabbath has been explained in Halachic terms: While we are to build the sanctuary six days a week, this work must cease on Shabbath. The text, however, presents a problem:

If Moshe has already prohibited all work on Shabbath, why single out the proscription of kindling a fire? This issue is addressed in Halachah as well as in our classic commentaries. Let us list their views:

Rashi quotes the two famous opinions in Halachah.[2] According to one, kindling a fire is forbidden separately to teach us that one who violates this law incurs lashes, not the death penalty. According to the other, the Torah is telling us that all thirty-nine forms of work prohibited on Shabbath should be treated individually. That is, if someone unwittingly performs several types of work on Shabbath, he must offer a sacrifice for each one.

Notably, while the first opinion clarifies why the Torah singles out fire, according to the second, any type of work mentioned separately would have sufficed. The latter therefore hardly explains why kindling a fire warrants special attention.

Ramban points out that, in verse 2, Moshe forbids "work," not "all work," so one may have deemed it permissible to cook, bake, and otherwise utilize fire to enhance his enjoyment of Shabbath. Therefore, the Torah explicitly prohibits fire, i.e., any use thereof.[3] (Incidentally, according to Ramban, this verse may be the source for the halachah that the Torah forbids cooking or baking on Shabbath only by means of fire, with other types of cooking proscribed only rabbinically.)

Finally, Sforno suggests that the Torah prohibits only constructive activities on Shabbath (destructive activities are forbidden only rabbinically.) Because fire is destructive, the Torah must therefore specifically ban its kindling.[4]

I should like to make a fresh start and view this matter contextually with one prefatory observation.

Others have noted that God commands Moshe first regarding the sanctuary, then concerning Shabbath.[5] However, when he transmits God's word to the Israelites, he speaks first of Shabbath, then of the sanctuary.[6]

My teacher, Rabbi Joseph B. Soloveitchik, attributed this reversal to the shattering transgression of the golden calf, which took place between God's communication to Moshe and his transmission of the Divine will to the people. Before this sin, one could speak to them of a sanctuary and all its theological implications. Axioms such as Shabbath could be left to the end as mere reminders of a fundamental truth. With the golden calf, though, it became apparent that the axioms of faith had to be reemphasized before any discussion of the sanctuary.

From this perspective, far more than simply restating the Shabbath principle, our text establishes the day as a bulwark against idolatry. The formulation of Shabbath becomes very

Fire as a Symbol

significant, particularly the emphasis upon the prohibition against kindling a fire.

This ban dramatically recalls the all-consuming conflagration into which the Israelites threw gold and out of which emerged the golden calf. Fire almost consumed the entire people — its future, its dreams, its whole history. It is as though Moshe were telling the children of Israel that, by constantly reminding themselves not to kindle fire on Shabbath, they will never again ignite the destructive flames of idolatry. This imagery reflects the Israelites' mood in the wake of their transgression.

The implications of our story extend to the foundations of Shabbath. Let us look at the matter from another perspective but within the same context.

Fire symbolizes man's technological advancement. Sforno points out that fire is necessary for all kinds of work.[7] Man's mastery of the physical world depends greatly upon the controlled use of fire in its many and varied forms. Therefore, more than any other prohibition, the ban on fire robs man of universal dominion. It underscores his limited ability versus God's unlimited, eternal rule.

When man believes he holds limitless power over the universe, he is flirting with idolatry. Conversely, if he recognizes his power as finite, the door to paganism is largely closed. Man is made passive on Shabbath to show the limits of his creativity. The prohibition against kindling fire reemphasizes that man is not omnipotent. Moshe singles out this proscription because this is the message he must convey following a transgression that at least bordered on idolatry.

These deductions provide us with a remarkable appreciation of a halachah derived from our verse: Courts may not administer physical punishment, such as lashes or death, on Shabbath.[8] *Sefer HaChinuch* suggests why: Even criminals should experience the restfulness of this day.[9]

In light of our analysis, this matter assumes a different

complexion. Shabbath guards against idolatry by restricting man's dominion. Nowhere is this limitation more necessary than in the judicial realm, in which man holds life and death in his hands. Indeed, a judge is called *elohim*, for he does the work of Elokim, the Supreme Judge. Therefore, he must not exercise his authority over his fellow man on Shabbath; otherwise, he is again just one step away from the inferno of idolatry.

1. Exod. 35:2.
2. Rashi, Exod. 35:3.
3. Ramban, Exod. 35:3.
4. Sforno, Exod. 35:3.
5. Note Exod. 25-31.
6. Note 35:1-4.
7. Sforno, Exod. 35:3.
8. *Yevamoth* 6b.
9. *Sefer HaChinuch, mitzvah* 114.

פרשת פקודי
Parashath Pekudei

REDEEMED

ויכס הענן את אהל מועד וכבוד ה׳ מלא את המשכן. ולא יכל משה לבוא אל אהל מועד כי שכן עליו הענן וכבוד ה׳ מלא את המשכן.

"THE CLOUD COVERED THE TENT OF MEETING, AND THE GLORY OF GOD FILLED THE TABERNACLE. AND MOSHE COULD NOT COME INTO THE TENT OF MEETING, FOR THE CLOUD RESTED UPON IT, AND THE GLORY OF GOD FILLED THE TABERNACLE." (Exodus 40:34-35)

These two verses bring us to the dramatic conclusion of the sanctuary episode, which started with the Divine directive to build a *mishkan*, continued with Moshe mobilizing the Israelites for this effort, and came to fruition with their contributions and the dedicated work of the artisans among them. As promised, God's glory now fills the tabernacle, and the Shechinah dwells among the Israelites.

Why the repetition of "and the glory of God filled the tabernacle," however? Ramban considers the sanctuary a portable Mount Sinai and attributes the redundancy to the mystical "glory" and "greatness" of that experience.[1] Other commentaries see in the repetition merely an expression of excitement and festive exaltation at the realization of the Divine presence.[2] There is a very simple alternative, but first several observations must be made.

The verses following our text state "And when the cloud was lifted from the tabernacle, the children of Israel journeyed on in all their journeys. And if the cloud would not rise, then they did not journey until the day it was lifted."[3] Essentially, all we want to know is that the tabernacle was built as specified, and God's presence was there. The journey hardly seems to matter here; it should be described elsewhere.

Finally we read, "For the cloud of God was over the tabernacle by day, and fire would be on it by night, before the eyes of the whole house of Israel throughout all their journeys."[4] The conjunction "for" implies that this verse explains what precedes it. How? Furthermore, why the use of the phrase "house of Israel" and not the much more common "children of Israel."

Our analysis will be based upon one passage in Ramban, which is crucial to understanding the theme and structure of the book of Exodus.

Though we call the second book of the Torah *Shemoth*, rabbinic literature refers to it as *The Book of Redemption*, on which basis it is also entitled Exodus. However, very little of the book deals with the liberation from Egypt. The remainder is devoted to revelation and the sanctuary. What, then, is implied by the names *The Book of Redemption* and Exodus?

In the introduction to his commentary on Exodus, Ramban explains that the entire book is about exodus. Leaving Egypt is merely the beginning of the Israelites' redemption. They must then receive the Torah and build the *mishkan* through which they experience the glory of God among them. Only then are they redeemed.

Ramban's definition of redemption is two-fold. One, the Israelites must return to their land. Two, they must reattain the spiritual status of the patriarchs. This means that God's glory must be with them constantly, as it was with the patriarchs. Bearing in mind these two principles, we can approach our text without resorting to mysticism.

(Incidentally, Ramban's criteria for redemption are simply those God outlined to Moshe. "I will take you out...I will save you...I will redeem you" refers to the departure from Egypt. "I will take you unto Me..." alludes to the revelation of the Torah through which the Israelites become bound to God. And "I will bring you to the land" speaks for itself.[5] These five expressions are all part of redemption. Hence Ramban's description of the structure and unity of Exodus.)

God has dwelled among *b'nei Yisrael* not just in the tabernacle. Both at the Red Sea and at Sinai, God was with them. But these were isolated incidents. God's *continuous* presence was realized only in the sanctuary. The repetition of "and the glory of God filled the tabernacle" merely underlines the constancy of the experience. Stated once, these words might have implied a fleeting phenomenon. By repeating them the Torah is telling us that it was permanent. God's glory rested upon the tabernacle even as it hovered over the tents of the patriarchs. This is one sign of redemption.

As for the second sign, entry into Eretz Yisrael, apparently just traveling toward the land fulfills this condition. The two verses quoted above, which indicate how the cloud of God directed the Israelites toward the promised land, therefore belong at the conclusion of Exodus, confirming that the redemption was complete.

The final verse of the book of Exodus remains to be clarified. How does this verse explain all that precedes it?

As mentioned, Ramban writes that redemption is complete when the Israelites regain the stature of the patriarchs. Our forefathers were "chariots of Divine glory," for that glory rested upon their tents constantly. As developed in a previous essay, holiness begins in the home. In fact, the holiness of the sanctuary derives from the holiness of the Jew. The materials built into the tabernacle first had to be sacred elements of the Jewish home.[6]

The Divine idea of the sanctuary took shape as it was transmitted to the craftsmen, who translated the notion of holiness into metal, wood, and other media. Conversely, the

Israelites elevated their physical homes to an abstract level of holiness. The glory of God dwelled in the sanctuary only because it dwelled in the home of each Jew.

Verse 38 now reads quite straightforwardly. God dwelled in the *mishkan*, so to speak, because "the cloud of God was... before the eyes of every *household* of Israel" as it was conceived both in theory and in practice at the time of the patriarchs.

1. Ramban, Exod. 25:1.
2. Cassuto, Exod. 40:34-38.
3. Exod. 40:36-37.
4. Exod. 40:38.
5. Exod. 6:6-8.
6. See *parashath Terumah*, "Holiness and Separation."

ספר ויקרא
Sefer VaYikra
The Book of Leviticus

פרשת ויקרא
Parashath VaYikra

THE OFFERING

ויקרא אל משה וידבר ה' אליו מאהל מועד לאמר. דבר אל בני ישראל ואמרת אלהם אדם כי יקריב מכם קרבן לה'....

"HE CALLED UNTO MOSHE; SPOKE UNTO HIM FROM THE TENT OF MEETING, SAYING: SPEAK UNTO THE CHILDREN OF ISRAEL; SAY UNTO THEM, 'IF ANY MAN OF YOU BRINGS AN OFFERING UNTO GOD....'" (Leviticus 1:1-2)

The opening of Leviticus deserves special attention. Its structure is, to say the least, unusual. It begins with the pronoun "He," referring only obliquely to God. In contrast, Moshe is mentioned explicitly. This pattern is then reversed: God is spelled out, while Moshe is referred to as "him."

Furthermore, when sacrifices are introduced in Leviticus, man is called *adam*. Though this appellation appears many times in the Torah, one must always account for the use of such a basic name — a name that returns us to Creation.

Finally, in the opening chapters of Leviticus, a book largely devoted to sacrifices, note the order in which the various offerings are treated: The *olah* (burnt offering) comes first, followed by the *minchah* (gift offering), the *shelamim* (peace offering), and the *chattath* (sin offering).[1] Perhaps this order is thematic.

These observations will lead us to formulate certain

principles of religious experience. No other book of the Torah deals so directly and so pointedly with these fundamental themes as does Leviticus. We shall begin, therefore, with a clear statement of the nature of the different expressions of religious experience and then note how they define the dimensions and moods of both our text and this book.

The two basic religious experiences are love and fear of God. No commentator describes these notions better than Rambam:

> And what is the path to love of Him and fear of Him? When man contemplates His deeds and His great and wondrous creations, and through them he perceives His infinite wisdom...man immediately loves and praises...and experiences a great desire to know the great Name.... And [even] as he thinks about these matters...he suddenly moves back and is afraid...knowing that he is a small, insignificant creature standing with negligible intelligence before the Omniscient. As David said: "For when I see Your heavens, the work of Your fingers.... What is man that You are mindful of him...?"[2]

Briefly, love of God goes hand in hand with a yearning to know and come close to Him. Through love, my existence is affirmed, my life gains meaning, and my potential becomes unbounded. When I love God, I come close to Him, and my being then has purpose.

Fear of God is the opposite phenomenon. When the full force of God's existence is revealed — to the degree that it can be — man senses his insignificance. He cringes before God's omnipotence and omniscience. Man's existence is negated; he feels meaningless. Such is fear of God.

Sacrifices suggest both experiences. While offerings are *chukkim*, inexplicable laws — as no less a rationalist than Rambam states[3] — a theme runs through this ritual. The root of the Hebrew word "*korban*" (sacrifice) means "come close."

The Offering

An offering therefore implies both approaching God and sacrificing all in His presence. The first act bespeaks love of God; the second, fear of God.

Two sacrifices in particular express these two ideas. The *shelamim* symbolizes the peaceful love of God. As the Midrash and Talmud point out, this offering signifies God and man co-existing in love, which tends to enhance and give meaning to man's existence.[4] On the other hand, the *chattath* reflects sinful man's worthlessness in the presence of the perfect God. The Almighty graciously accepts the sacrifice of an animal instead of a human being.[5] Nevertheless, the *chattath* conveys man's insignificance: He cringes before God in dread. In contrast, the *shelamim* affirms man's value: He stands before God, yearning to know and merge with Him.

Thus, the series of sacrifices recorded in the earliest chapters of Leviticus mirrors the human soul turning to God and experiencing His presence:

First there is an *olah*, a burning desire to become one with God, to be consumed by Him, as Rambam suggests in the text quoted above. This is man's first reaction to God. But this yearning is concretized in a *minchah*, a gift. Man approaches God carefully, deliberately, with a gift. Only then comes the *shelamim*, the peaceful basking in God's presence.

No sooner is this state reached, though, than man suddenly moves back (to paraphrase Rambam) and deems himself so infinitesimal and saturated with sin that he must offer a *chattath*. With this sacrifice, the cycle of attraction and repulsion is complete.

The term *adam* depicts these dynamics of the human soul: *Adam* is commonly derived from the word "*adamah*," earth, emphasizing man's insignificance. Man is earth, fashioned out of dust, and his existence — if it can even be called that — is ephemeral. Before the eternal, omnipotent, and omniscient God, this existence is negated. *Adam* is *adamah* and nothing more.

The Depths of Simplicity

However, as Netziv writes, *adam* has a different root: *domeh*, emulate.[6] For man can emulate God and come close to Him in great love, thereby affirming his existence. The same term *adam*, which has just been interpreted as *adamah*, suddenly acquires the meaning *adameh*, I will be like Him.

Therefore, in instituting sacrifices, the Torah describes man as *adam*. This word succinctly and unequivocally embodies the magnificent dynamic of the sensitive soul — attraction and repulsion — as symbolized by sacrifices. From the *olah* through the *shelamim*, man exemplifies *adameh*, I yearn to resemble Him, only to recognize that he is but *adamah*, steeped in sin in the very presence of God.

We can now return to the first verse of Leviticus. Though brief and simple, this verse, expresses the spectrum of religious experience. Its first word, "*vayikra*" (He called), is a term of endearment.[7] Yet the verse continues with "*vayedabber*" (He spoke), which is much more rigorous. *Dibbur* demands man's subservience.

Similarly, in the first phrase of this verse, God's name is hidden, and Moshe stands out. In the second phrase, God's name is distinct, while Moshe is concealed in a pronoun. For man's first religious experience is one of love, and his existence — as Moshe's — is affirmed. But man's second experience is fear, and, in the overwhelming power of God's *dibbur*, his existence — as Moshe's — is negated.

---

1. Lev. 1-4.
2. *Mishneh Torah*, "*Hilchoth Yesodei HaTorah*" 2:2, based on Psalms 8:4-5.
3. Ibid., "*Hilchoth Me'ilah*" 8:8.
4. Note Ramban, Gen. 46:1.
5. Ramban, Lev. 1:9.
6. *Ha'amek Davar*, Gen. 1:26.
7. Rashi, Lev. 1:1.

פרשת צו
Parashath Tzav

The Burning Altar

וידבר ה' אל משה לאמר. צו את אהרן ואת בניו לאמר זאת תורת העלה הוא העלה על מוקדה על המזבח כל הלילה עד הבקר ואש המזבח תוקד בו. ולבש הכהן מדו בד ומכנסי בד ילבש על בשרו....

"GOD SPOKE UNTO MOSHE, SAYING: COMMAND AHARON AND HIS SONS, SAYING, 'THIS IS THE TEACHING OF THE BURNT OFFERING: IT IS THE BURNT OFFERING ON THE FIREWOOD ON THE ALTAR ALL NIGHT UNTIL THE MORNING, AND THE FIRE OF THE ALTAR SHALL BE KEPT BURNING UPON IT. THE PRIEST SHALL WEAR HIS LINEN GARMENT, AND HIS LINEN BREECHES SHALL HE WEAR UPON HIS FLESH....'" (Leviticus 6:1-3)

A word of introduction is in order before exploring this Torah portion. Symbolic Biblical interpretation is fraught with danger. Generally, Torah analysis is guided and restrained by the simple meaning of words and phrases. Based as well on our rich Midrashic and Talmudic literature and our classic commentaries, one can safely apply his religious sensibility and dimensions. Symbolism removes all these barriers, however. Suddenly, anything can symbolize anything. But the very freedom of this interpretation turns it into little more than pure fancy. We must therefore recognize our limitations when employing this method of Torah study.

Nonetheless, symbolism has two redeeming features. First, if symbolism is suggested in our Midrashic literature or in other authoritative sources, then we can comfortably resort to them. Second, if the symbolist intends to awaken the soul to a great issue or an epic drama, then his effort is certainly worthwhile. The following symbolic essay contains both these features. It is based on *Or HaChayim*,[1] though with several minor changes and major diversions in emphasis and scope. Additionally, it dramatizes the condition of *knesseth Yisrael* and the dynamics of its history, which peaked in 1967 with the Six-Day War.

Tzav starts with the *olah* — not the voluntary burnt offering, but the obligatory one brought each day. While one such obligatory offering is brought in the morning and another in the afternoon, our text begins with an *olah* already consumed throughout the night.

Furthermore, the priest is not even mentioned until he comes to take up the ashes. He removes them from the altar, changes clothes, and then carries the ashes out to a "*makom tahor*," a clean place.[2]

Next, the text repeats the burning of the fire,[3] which seems rather important in this passage. Such emphasis upon burning should attract our attention and spark our imagination.

Another *olah* follows and then the *shelamim*, the peace offering.[4] Why this order? No sacrifice may be brought before the morning *olah*, but the first sacrifice to follow it need not be a *shelamim*. Rashi offers several interpretations.[5]

Finally, Scripture repeats that the fire — the continuous fire — shall burn on the altar and not be extinguished.[6] Noting this repetition, Rashi offers the Talmudic interpretation of the verse: The fire of the candelabrum is continuous; this fire comes from the altar.[7] While Rashi's is a Halachic translation, its imagery can move a Jewish soul.

Again, we are not interpreting, we are using these phrases to paint a picture of Jewish history and suffering, which suggests eschatology and captures the heartbeat of our people.

The Burning Altar

As mentioned, our major ideas and symbolism come from *Or HaChayim*.

This portion is nothing less than the story of Israel's suffering and redemption. All through the night, a *moked*, a conflagration, consumes Israel. One gigantic furnace devours the *olah*, with a priest nowhere to be found. In our Midrashic literature, the *kohen*, the priest, often symbolizes God, the *kohen* of Israel. During this long, dark night, the *kohen* cannot be seen or heard. One wonders whether He sees the furnace or whether He is at all concerned with this destructive conflagration and with the *olah* it mercilessly consumes.

Though it looks like a *moked* — like one wild, pitiless furnace — upon careful examination, the "fire of the altar [that is] kept burning"[8] becomes apparent. An invisible *kohen* permits the furnace to incinerate, but a meaningful, holy fire is growing. The furnace becomes an altar, the *moked* a *mizbeiach*. And somehow, we reach out to a brighter morning and a more purposeful tomorrow. With no excuses and no understanding of the interminable, dreadful night, we find that suddenly the *kohen* has appeared!

His garments are linen, the fabric of *chessed*, of mercy. Compassionately, the *kohen* takes the ashes, the residue of the furnace and the altar, lifts these charred remains, and sanctifies them. With them, he will rebuild what the furnace has consumed. God appears here both as the merciful Father of the ashes and as the vengeful King, who will punish those responsible for the fire and its destruction.

The *kohen* changes clothes and takes the ashes to a "clean place." *Or HaChayim* insists that this place is Eretz Yisrael. Thus, the remnant of the people that has survived the furnace is brought to the Holy Land, and given new life and a new perspective. But the battle is far from over. The *kohen*, the king of this people, realizes a continuous *olah*, but there is no *moked*, no furnace, only an altar. Every sacrifice is holy, for it is dedicated to realizing the dreams, hopes, and future

133

of the people. The *kohen* now offers a new type of *olah*, an offering intended to secure the land and its boundaries and safeguard it as the home of the people. To this end, there are more sacrifices, more *oloth* — but the goal is to bring the *shelamim*, the peace offering.

On this altar, sacrifices are still being offered; those who designed and perfected the furnace seek to rebuild it. But *knesseth Yisrael* now sacrifices on an altar conceived to bring *shelamim* — to bring harmony to its people and neighbors.

This is hardly the story's end. In the End of Days, Israel will yet teach mankind about God and *chessed*, two principles for which our nation stands.

Rambam writes, "And at that time, there will be no hunger or war, and the concern of the whole world will be only to know God...therefore the Jews will be recognized as wise men who know the great secrets"[9] of God's existence as well as man can. Israel will then teach humanity theology and *chessed*. Indeed, the menorah becomes extremely symbolic, for the light of knowledge and truth will shine forth from Israel and illuminate mankind.

How beautifully this passage concludes that the fire on the altar shall not be consumed, but, as Rashi points out, it shall illuminate the menorah,[10] enlightening mankind.

What is particularly significant and magnificent in the imagery of this entire story is that it transports us from a *moked* to a *mizbeiach* to a menorah — from a furnace to an altar to a candelabrum.

1. *Or HaChayim*, Lev. 6:2.
2. Lev. 6:3-4.
3. Ibid. 6:5.
4. Ibid.
5. Rashi, Lev. 6:5.
6. Lev. 6:6.
7. Rashi, Lev. 6:6.
8. Lev. 6:6.
9. *Mishneh Torah*, "*Hilchoth Melachim*" 12:5.
10. Rashi, Lev. 6:6.

פרשת שמיני
Parashath Shemini

Bricks of Sapphire

ויקחו בני אהרן נדב ואביהוא איש מחתתו ויתנו בהן אש וישימו עליה קטרת ויקריבו לפני ה' אש זרה אשר לא צוה אתם.

"THE SONS OF AHARON, NADAV AND AVIHU, TOOK EACH MAN HIS CENSER, PUT FIRE IN THEM, PUT INCENSE THEREON, [AND] OFFERED STRANGE FIRE BEFORE GOD, WHICH HE HAD NOT COMMANDED THEM." (Leviticus 10:1)

Our *pasuk* describes the transgression of Aharon's sons, and the following verse informs us, "Fire issued forth from God and consumed them — and they died before God."[1] The text does not clarify their sin. This subject has therefore become popular in Midrashic writings as well as in our classic Torah commentaries. Let us list the more common interpretations.

Rashi cites Midrashic traditions that Nadav and Avihu either rendered Halachic decisions in the presence of their teachers, Moshe and Aharon, or entered the sanctuary intoxicated.[2] Since Scripture does not mention these transgressions, we must search other Torah sources to substantiate these opinions.

Sforno reads the text literally and maintains simply that Nadav and Avihu offered incense, which they had not been commanded to do.[3] This approach may connect with the Midrashic contention that they made Halachic decisions improperly. In any event, Sforno's interpretation is close to the text. Rashbam's is even closer, for it regards the "fire" — a strange fire — as the heart of the crime.[4]

Following his theory about the groups associated with Korach's rebellion, Netziv argues that, in their overwhelming desire to come close to God in great and all-consuming love, Nadav and Avihu offered incense beyond the bounds of Halachah.[5] This error teaches us that expressions of love for God — however noble — must be guided by the hard and fast principles of Jewish law. Significantly, Netziv insists that the fundamental piety of Aharon's sons goes unchallenged. Although many modern commentaries and preachers have unfortunately taken them as common criminals, God considered them "*krovai* — My near and dear ones."[6]

Ramban writes, "they set incense on the fire, as Scripture has stated, 'they shall place incense for Your anger,'[7] and they directed their attention only to this."[8] How does this comment explain their crime? Apparently paraphrasing Ramban, Rabbeinu Bachya says that they followed only God's *middath hadin*, His attribute of justice, ignoring His attribute of mercy. These observations are mystical, yet they can be meaningful to us.

If we examine the content of Nadav and Avihu's transgression, we find that it occurred on the day Aharon was to begin his service in the sanctuary, which would cause God's glory to dwell both therein and among the people. Indeed, although our *pasuk* begins a new chapter (Leviticus 10), such divisions are gentile in origin, whereas the text itself treats our story and Aharon's as one. Here a word of explanation is in order.

In the Torah's account of Aharon's initiation into the service of the sanctuary, there is a sense of urgency, because — according to our Midrashic literature — God's glory did not appear as rapidly as the people had expected.[9] The Torah describes the inaugural offerings, Aharon's blessing the people, his and Moshe's entering the sanctuary, and finally their unexplained emergence to bless the people again.[10] As Rashi notes, the charged atmosphere and frenzied activity betray a concern that, after all the sacrifices, there was no sign of Divine acceptance or glory.

Sensing that something must be done for the people, Moshe and Aharon enter the sanctuary and appeal for Divine mercy. The brothers then emerge and bless the people again, attempting to elevate their spirit, and reassure them that God will be with them and answer their prayers. They are in no way blamed for the absence of the Divine presence. On the contrary, Aharon and Moshe assume responsibility. Here the transgression of Aharon's sons becomes so real that it is almost cruel. (Of course, this "cruelty" is from their perspective, not ours. We are only translating, not judging.)

Nadav and Avihu appear in a related Torah episode.[11] As they accompanied Moshe, Aharon, and seventy of the elders of Israel up Mount Sinai, "They saw the God of Israel and, under His feet, a kind of sapphire brick and the essence of the heavens for purity."[12] Though they saw all this, God did not punish them: "They saw Elokim, [and] they ate and drank."[13] Based on the Midrash, Rashi maintains that Nadav and Avihu looked too intently upon God, but, in order not to mar the festivity of the covenant, God punished them only later, in our episode. Obviously there is some relationship between these two incidents.

Ramban compares what Aharon's sons saw to Yechezkel's celebrated first prophecy. He, too, glimpsed the purity of the heavens, something like sapphire, above it a throne, and, above it all, a vision of God.[14] Strikingly, though, Nadav and Avihu beheld these images in the opposite order. Yechezkel looked up, while Aharon's sons looked down. This difference in perspective is the essence of our story.

Yechezkel, Nadav, and Avihu all view God's relationship to Israel's often tragic history. Yechezkel, however, sees it as a human being, while Nadav and Avihu observe it — almost like angels — from above. Looking upward from the midst of tragedy, Yechezkel perceives the heavens opening, sees the vision of God, falls in prostration, and prays that the Almighty temper His attribute of justice. Viewing the experience from above, Nadav and Avihu see Elokim, the truth of Divine justice, and they can even eat and drink. There is a Midrashic tradition that they saw the sapphire brick as a replica of the bricks the Israelites made in Egypt.[15] The brick appeared to them as beautiful sapphire because they felt they understood God's justice. Looking downward, they saw history the way God sees it — and the "brick" is indeed sapphire. Yechezkel does not presume such comprehension of *middath hadin*.

When Moshe and Aharon see that the sanctuary services have gone unanswered, in the spirit of Yechezkel, they refuse to admit defeat. They pray, offer blessings, and beg for mercy. They repeatedly bless the people, lift their spirits, and assure them that God will respond to their prayers.

Nadav and Avihu note only the impact of *middath hadin* — and they immediately make peace with it. The people are simply unworthy of God's presence, they reason, due to the sin of the golden calf or some other offense. All they can do, think the sons of Aharon, is offer incense. As Ramban often points out, incense appeases *middath hadin* but reflects full recognition thereof.

In short, Nadav and Avihu react to the tension of the day by presuming to understand Divine justice and the reason for God's anger. Once again, they see a "brick" of sapphire. But when people are suffering, such complacency seems cruel.

1. Lev. 10:2.
2. Rashi, Lev. 10:2.
3. Sforno, Lev. 10:1.

4. Rashbam, Lev. 10:1.
5. *Ha'amek Davar*, Lev. 10:1.
6. Lev. 10:3.
7. Dev. 33:10. Regarding this translation, see Ramban, Exod. 30:1.
8. Ramban, Lev. 10:2.
9. Note Rashi, Lev. 9:23.
10. Lev. 9.
11. See Rashi, Exod. 24:10.
12. Exod. 24:9-10.
13. Ibid. 24:11.
14. Ramban, Exod. 24:10, based on Ezek. 1.
15. Note Rashi, Exod. 24:10.

פרשת תזריע
Parashath Tazria

THE DRAMA OF BIRTH

דבר אל בני ישראל לאמר אשה כי תזריע וילדה זכר וטמאה שבעת ימים כימי נדת דותה תטמא.

"SPEAK UNTO THE CHILDREN OF ISRAEL, SAYING: IF A WOMAN BECOMES PREGNANT AND BEARS A MALE, SHE SHALL BE IMPURE SEVEN DAYS; LIKE THE SEPARATION DAYS OF HER BEING UNWELL SHALL SHE BE IMPURE." (Leviticus 12:2)

Let us set down the Halachic stipulations indicated in this *pasuk* and those that follow, so that we may have a clearer picture of what the Torah is telling us here. After giving birth to a boy, a woman is impure seven days, whether or not there has been the usual sign of impurity, i.e., blood. On the eighth day, the child is to be circumcised.[1] Incidentally, it is rather strange that this *mitzvah* is recorded here among the laws of a new mother.

After the seven impure days come thirty-three "pure" days.[2] During this period, the mother is considered pure and thus permitted to have relations with her husband. Her purity is unaffected by any issue of blood. Whereas, for the first seven days, she is impure even if she does not discharge blood, during these thirty-three days, she is pure even if she does. (It should be noted that we are describing Torah law alone. One should not draw any conclusions regarding our practice, which involves many rabbinic injunctions.) Nonetheless, she may not enter the sanctuary or partake of any holy food.³

At the conclusion of this forty-day process, the woman brings two sacrifices: an *olah* (burnt offering) and a *chattath* (sin offering).⁴ She may then enter the sanctuary.

We shall concentrate on these laws, though those accompanying the birth of a female differ somewhat. These ordinances are probably *chukkim*, so their rationale is elusive. Yet the total of forty days has been associated with a child's formation during the first forty days following conception. Since a sin offering is prescribed, indicating some form of transgression, we must examine this drama with care. We shall study it on two levels, one psychological and one religious.

Both psychologically and familially, childbirth is an experience of almost shattering proportions. A new personality has entered the family constellation, and all relationships therein must be redefined. The halachoth of childbirth largely determine these relationships.

A woman who gives birth changes both physically and mentally — and she is not always happy with these changes. She needs time to concentrate on herself.⁵ Not only must she evaluate and accept her transformation, she must recognize it as a fulfillment of herself as a woman. Thus, the Halachah gives her seven days to be by herself, reflect on her purpose in life, and appreciate the mission she has fulfilled.

Additionally, a relationship has been formed between mother and infant. Need one be a psychologist to acknowledge the strong bonds of love and concern uniting mother and child? Yet authorities in many fields have emphasized that a mother must recognize her baby's independence. Even at birth, she must realize that this infant will eventually grow up, set out on his own, and build a life for himself. All her love, concern, and identification must not blind her to this truth. Hence the inclusion of circumcision here. For this act affirms that he is a member of a people and will become a father in his own right some day.

Most important perhaps is the relationship between the mother and her husband. A new baby requires attention, love, and care. Lest these responsibilities infringe on a marriage, the Torah designates thirty-three days during which the mother is considered pure and may reestablish her relationship with her husband. At this time, she may not enter the sanctuary — she must not involve herself with religious and communal institutions. Rather, she should focus on reaffirming this most intimate bond, around which her family is built.

Forty days is indeed required to form a personality. However, this parallel refers not to the newborn but to the mother. During these forty days, she evolves into a new woman — able to live with herself, love her new child and recognize his individuality, and love her husband, with whom her family life is complete.

Another dimension of this story cannot be overlooked. The Midrash repeatedly stresses the miracles of conception, pregnancy, and birth.[6] In this drama, man and woman participate in an act of creation. In Deuteronomy, the Torah notes that, once the Israelites conquer and build up their land, they may attribute their prosperity to themselves and abandon God. The Torah then emphasizes that God alone empowers man to achieve all these wonders.[7] Likewise, when the Torah treats man's most fundamental act of creativity — the creation of another human being — we receive a similar warning in the form of the laws we are considering.

The mother of a newborn spends seven days, perhaps, praying that her physical functions return to normal. Her child's circumcision indicates that his conception and birth are holy and express God's will. And she offers sacrifices in thanksgiving for the miracle God has wrought. Man and woman become partners with God in creation — but they dare not forget Him.

The sacrifices themselves are particularly interesting. Both the *olah* and the *chattath* are offered, reflecting the Torah's attitude toward sexuality. Without entering into a definitive discussion of this matter, suffice it to say that the Torah sees in physical intimacy the potential for both the greatest holiness and and the worst depravity. Halachically regulated, man's sexual activity expresses partnership with the Divine in the act of creation. Unbridled, however, sex degrades man to the level of animals. In his *Mishneh Torah*, Rambam includes these laws within "The Book of Holiness."

Man is imperfect. The Torah, relate our rabbis, was given not to angels but to frail humans. Accordingly, no sexual activity can be devoid of personal pleasure and directed wholly to the service of God.

That's why a woman who has just given birth offers both an *olah*, expressing all-consuming devotion to God, and a *chattath*, a sin offering. For while the sexual act has made her and her husband partners with God in creation, it also inevitably, if paradoxically, contains an element void of His service.

1. Lev. 12:3.
2. Ibid. 12:4.
3. Ibid.
4. Ibid. 12:6.
5. Note Sforno, Lev. 12:7.
6. Note *Lev. Rabbah* 14.
7. Deut. 8:7-18.

פרשת מצורע
Parashath Metzora

Slander

...וכפר עליו הכהן לפני ה'. ועשה הכהן את החטאת וכפר על המטהר מטמאתו ואחר ישחט את העלה. והעלה הכהן את העלה ואת המנחה המזבחה וכפר עליו הכהן וטהר.

"...AND THE PRIEST SHALL ATONE FOR HIM BEFORE GOD. THE PRIEST SHALL OFFER THE *CHATTATH*, HE SHALL ATONE FOR HIM WHO IS PURIFYING HIMSELF OF HIS IMPURITY, AND AFTERWARD HE SHALL SLAUGHTER THE *OLAH*. THE PRIEST SHALL OFFER UP THE *OLAH* AND THE *MINCHAH* UPON THE ALTAR — THE PRIEST SHALL ATONE FOR HIM, AND HE BECOMES PURE."
(Leviticus 14:18-20)

Because the laws of the *metzora*, the leper, are highly technical and complex, we shall concern ourselves with his purification process as outlined above.

A *metzora* offers three sacrifices: an *asham*, offered for a transgression; a *chattath*, also offered following a sin; and finally an *olah*, a burnt offering unassociated with wrongdoing.

Classic commentaries discuss the purpose of these sacrifices and are particularly interested in the threefold atonement mentioned in our text. Notably, the priest "...atones for [the *metzora*] before God," "atones for him who is purifying himself," and "...shall atone for him, and he becomes pure." This repeated atonement demands explanation.

Ramban maintains that the *asham* atones for the sin of slander, *lashon hara*, a transgression punished by leprosy. The *chattath* atones for the leper's potential reaction to his suffering. For his suffering and subsequent isolation may lead him to curse God and question His justice. The *olah*, in contrast, merely purifies the *metzora*, enabling him to return home to normalcy.[1]

Netziv echoes Ramban but asserts that the *olah* atones for mental offenses, for thought generally precedes action or speech.[2]

Interestingly, while atonement is indeed mentioned three times, the phraseology differs in each case. These distinctions touch upon very significant elements of the human personality, which are reflected in the sin of slander.

In Rambam's *Mishneh Torah*, after stating that slander invites leprosy, the author writes:

> And this is the nature of the council of evil scorners. First they indulge in meaningless words.... And by doing so they come to relay the disgrace of the righteous.... And by doing so, they will develop a habit of speaking against the prophets, casting doubts on their words.... And by doing so, they come to speak against God and deny the essence [of Judaism, i.e., His existence]....[3]

The crux of slander is the second stage. When the wicked denigrate the righteous, we are on the threshold of slander. In effect, "the righteous" could refer to any target of slander. For slander is a process of cause and effect. The first stage is the cause, the second, the "slander," and the third, the ultimate result. This syndrome can be explained psychologically.

Slander against the righteous, as Rambam calls *lashon hara*, begins with self-deprecation. When a person loses faith in his own stature, he strikes out against others. If I see nothing good or valuable in myself, I will very probably see no good in others. Conversely, my appreciation of others stems from my appreciation of myself. Two sources stress this notion:

The Mishnah in *Avoth* reads, "Who is honored? He who honors others,"[4] implying that only the one who recognizes his own honor and worth can honor and respect his fellow man. One classic commentary suggests that only such an individual *can afford* to honor others.[5] Conversely, one who denies his own value slanders others.

Similarly, from Rashi's famous comment on the verse "You shall not take revenge or bear a grudge against the children of your people; love your neighbor as yourself...,"[6] we must conclude that one who violates either of these proscriptions betrays low self-esteem. Although a vengeful person seems to fail only in dealing with others, his weakness lies within. He cannot fulfill the end of the verse, "love your neighbor as yourself," because he does not love himself.

Rambam thus describes a group of people with no purpose in life, who consequently waste their time. Such behavior inevitably lowers one's self-worth immeasurably and leads to slander. Understandably, jealousy creeps into this slander. After all, the righteous are concerned with important matters — they are in the mainstream of life, involved in creative or productive activity. Therefore, the wicked must resort to slander in order to depreciate them.

It is then only a step from an inferiority complex to a compensatory superiority complex. This arrogant attempt to build oneself up is tantamount to idolatry or, at least, to denying God's existence. The cycle is then complete: from self-deprecation to slander and to idolatry.

Such is Rambam's analysis of *lashon hara* — roots, transgression, and ultimate result. Astonishingly, the purification process follows this structure:

The Torah first insists that the leper offer an *asham*, generally more demanding than a *chattath*, to atone for his ultimate denial of God, which, according to Rambam, results from slander. Hence the stress on "...aton[ing] for him *before God.*"

He must then bring a *chattath*, the usual sin offering, which atones for the slander itself. That is, it "atones for him who is purifying himself *of his impurity.*"

Now we approach the key to the purification process. If this procedure is to stop the cycle we have described, the problem must be attacked at its roots. And slander is rooted in the slanderer's self-image. We must build him up, teaching him his own worth, stature, and purpose. Hence the *olah* (literally, "ascend"), which elevates the individual by illustrating his potential to come close to God and endow his life with meaning. Such a sense of self makes slander unnecessary if not impossible. Significantly, the text now reads, "...the priest shall atone for him, and he shall be pure."

1. Ramban, Lev. 14:18.
2. *Ha'amek Davar,* Lev. 14:20.
3. *"Hilchoth Tumath Tzoraath"* 16:10.
4. *Avoth* 4:1.
5. *Ruach Chayim, Avoth* 4:1.
6. Lev. 19:18.

פרשת אחרי מות
Parashath Acharei Moth

Laws and Statutes

דבר אל בני ישראל ואמרת אלהם אני ה' אלקיכם. כמעשה ארץ מצרים אשר ישבתם בה לא תעשו וכמעשה ארץ כנען אשר אני מביא אתכם שמה לא תעשו ובחקתיהם לא תלכו.

"SPEAK UNTO THE CHILDREN OF ISRAEL; SAY UNTO THEM, 'I AM THE LORD, YOUR GOD. ACCORDING TO THE DEEDS OF THE LAND OF EGYPT, WHERE YOU SOJOURNED, YOU SHALL NOT DO, AND ACCORDING TO THE DEEDS OF THE LAND OF CANAAN, UNTO WHICH I BRING YOU, YOU SHALL NOT DO, AND IN THEIR STATUTES YOU SHALL NOT WALK.'"

(Leviticus 18:2-3)

So fundamental are these verses to Torah philosophy that we shall analyze them phrase by phrase.

"I am the Lord, your God" is repeated often in this section of Leviticus and stands out as the basis of all commandments. Here, however, rather than following a directive as it normally does, it opens an entire Torah portion. Apparently noting this anomaly, the Midrash proposes that the phrase implies two things: "I am the One who spoke, and the world came into being," i.e., "I am the Creator"; and "I am all-merciful."[1] How do these ideas introduce the subject discussed at hand?

Furthermore, the text warns first against the deeds of Egypt, then against the deeds of Canaan. According to Rashi, though, Canaanite practices were more detestable than Egyptian ones. Logic would therefore dictate that Canaanite rites be banned before their Egyptian counterparts (in keeping with the Talmudic principle, "*lo zu af zu*" [not only this but even that]).

Next, in verse 4, the Israelites are told, "Do My laws and guard My statutes...." Why these different verbs?

Additionally, in verse 5, "do" again refers to laws, and "guard" to statutes. Yet they read as one continuous phrase. Rashi maintains that the text thereby relates both "guarding" and "doing" to both laws and statutes.[2] Something very important is communicated here, and we must clarify these terms.

These verses introduce numerous laws and statutes covering every interest and activity — intimacy, economics, relationships, and communal responsibilities. Moreover, in these ordinances, one detects a theme of "freedom." By observing them, man becomes a free agent, liberated from physical, economic, and social pressures. The dramatic and all-embracing conclusion is that "the children of Israel...are My servants,"[3] — not the servants of any other person or drive.

When one people subjugates another, the latter's adoption of the former's laws signifies spiritual enslavement. Yet so does the conqueror's emulation of the conquered. Thus, the Torah commands the Israelites: Ignore the practices of the Egyptians, who ruled over you, and reject even the customs of the Canaanites, over whom you rule.

We must now define "*mishpatim* — laws" and "*chukkim* — statutes."

Rashi[4] explains that *mishpatim* are commandments whose objective is clear. Their value is unquestionable. *Mishpatim* generally control interpersonal relationships and are intended to create a harmonious and peaceful society.

On the other hand, the reasons for *chukkim* are unclear and somewhat mystical. It's not that these statutes have no rationales — they simply are unrevealed to us. Typically, *chukkim* govern one's relationship with God.

We observed above that the Torah pairs the verbs "do" and "guard" with laws and statutes, respectively. What do these terms mean? Rambam emphasizes that, although we do not understand *chukkim*, we should neither assume they have no reason nor consider them less important than *mishpatim*.[5] (Incidentally, in this text, Rambam deems all sacrifices *chukkim*, despite his famous rationalization in *Guide for the Perplexed*.)[6] He then quotes our verse and defines its verbs. Doing, of course, means observing or performing. Guarding says Rambam, means valuing even seemingly without reason. Therefore, the challenge of laws is to do them, whereas the challenge of statutes is to guard them.

There is no difficulty recognizing the value and purpose of *mishpatim*. Such laws are self-explanatory, and every civilized individual holds them in the highest regard. However, their performance can be quite trying, since other people are involved. Accordingly, the Torah says, "Do My laws...," for we will certainly guard them, but we must observe them as well.

In contrast, *chukkim* are easily observed. After all, no other individual is affected. The challenge, then, is to esteem them as genuine religious experiences. Thus God seems to say in the Torah, "I presume you will 'do' My statutes, but I insist that you guard them as well."

In verse 5, the Torah pointedly reemphasizes the unity of all Divine commandments. Though we have discussed laws and statutes separately, we must recognize that they are one. Laws without statutes or vice versa does not reflect the totality of the Torah or of Jewish life. Hence the seemingly random intermingling of various laws and statutes in succeeding sections of Leviticus.

One final point about "...I am the Lord, your God"[7] and the Midrash's two explanations: God as Creator and God as the essence of mercy.[8] Midrashim often relate *chukkim* to the laws of heaven and earth, contending that our observance of the Torah's statutes somehow upholds the very structure of creation. Indeed, Ramban writes that planting "mixtures" and crossbreeding animals are forbidden for such acts tamper with categories of creation.[9] On the other hand, *mishpatim* are to engender compassion. God therefore identifies Himself both ways here.

1. *Lev. Rabbah, Sifra, parashah* 9a.
2. Rashi, Lev. 18:5.
3. Lev. 25:55.
4. Rashi, Lev. 18:4.
5. *Mishneh Torah, "Hilchoth Me'ilah"* 8:8.
6. *Moreh Nevuchim,* pt. III, ch. 32.
7. Lev. 18:4.
8. *Lev. Rabbah, Sifra, parashah* 9a.
9. Ramban, Lev. 19:19.

פרשת קדשים
Parashath Kedoshim

BE HOLY

דבר אל כל עדת בני ישראל ואמרת אלהם קדשים תהיו כי קדוש אני ה׳ אלקיכם.

"SPEAK UNTO THE WHOLE CONGREGATION OF THE CHILDREN OF ISRAEL; SAY UNTO THEM, 'YOU SHALL BE HOLY, FOR I, THE LORD, YOUR GOD, AM HOLY.'" (Leviticus 19:2)

The expression "*kedoshim tihyu* — be holy" is crucial not only to this portion but to the structure of the Torah. This directive must be defined, for it is addressed to the "whole congregation." Significantly, holiness is unreserved for any section of the Jewish people; it is expected of and accessible to all.

Rashi interprets "*kedoshim tihyu*" as "be separated from prohibited sexual relations and from transgression."[1] The commentaries on Rashi explain that "transgression," too, refers to violation of the Torah's sexual mores.[2]

Ramban notes that the text states merely, "be separate," without specifying any sin. Hence his famous theory:[3] While the Torah restricts man in many ways, there is sufficient room for all types of excesses. In fact, man has such freedom that he may indulge in various pleasurable activities to the exclusion of spiritual/intellectual pursuits, which are his special domain as a human being created "in God's image."[4] Man can thus become what Ramban calls "a despicable character with the Torah's permission"[5] if all his indulgences violate no law.

To prevent this eventuality, the Torah commands us, "Be holy...," meaning: Refrain from self-gratification even where technically permitted. This is Ramban's understanding of "*kedoshim tihyu.*"

Although Ramban's interpretation is very popular, I have a simple question: Why didn't the Torah formulate its prohibitions such that there would be no need to exhort us, "Be holy..."? Surely its proscriptions could have been codified to preclude the possibility of "a despicable character with the Torah's permission." Of course, a certain flexibility is necessary to provide for different personalities and idiosyncrasies. However, this is not the whole answer.

To capture the flavor of Ramban's theory, one must study his complete comment. It does not end with his translation of "Be holy...." Rather, he proceeds to explain how the Torah formulates its injunctions. He offers two examples, which complement our verse. The Torah bans various labors on Shabbath and then adds a general commandment, "you shall rest,"[6] thereby discouraging activity that violates no prohibitions but should nonetheless be avoided on this holy day. Similarly, the Torah forbids theft, usury, false testimony, dishonesty in business, etc., and then insists, "You shall do what is right and good...."[7] This generalization, too, precludes various forms of exploitation, even though no prohibition is involved.

Given this pattern, particularly in three areas — man's physical gratification, his relationship with God as reflected in Shabbath, and his relationship with his fellow man — we must deduce its underlying concept.

Ramban emphasizes that all proscriptions can be circumvented. That is why the Torah does not include all cases: It cannot, for one can always find a loophole.

There is, however, one way to prevent this perversion of the law. While prohibitions can be circumvented, "positive" precepts cannot. When all restrictions are conceptualized in one affirmative notion, devious, underhanded violations are unlikely. The letter of the law can be tampered with but not the spirit.

There is yet another, very significant illustration of this idea. "Positive" commandments generally require a religious article, such as *tzitzith, tefillin,* an *ethrog, matzah,* or a *shofar.* "Negative" commandments do not. Therefore, all three of the aforementioned categories revolve around no "*mitzvah* object." Only the general "positive" commandment in each case posits such an "object," through which all the prohibitions become realized. That "object" is man himself.

Let us examine the three areas. The bans on various forms of sexual activity are intended to fashion a "holy" personality. The injunctions against work on Shabbath are designed to foster belief in God and Creation. The general "positive" commandment to rest gives direction to all these proscriptions: Man, himself an "article of *mitzvah,*" is to become a believer. And the prohibitions of theft, slander, and dishonesty may be very technical, but "You shall do what is right and good" instructs man to become an honest friend.

Interestingly, these three realms, where the Torah attempts to transform man into an "article of *mitzvah,*" include the three cardinal sins: adultery, idolatry, and murder.[8] For wherever the ultimate transgressions are so basic, restrictions must be strengthened and given purpose by "positive" commandments.

Perhaps this idea underlies Rashi's interpretation of "Be holy..." as "be separated from prohibited sexual relations and from transgression." While "transgression" certainly denotes the violation of a specific prohibition, "be separated" may imply the overall directive to shape man into an "article of *mitzvah.*"

THE DEPTHS OF SIMPLICITY

1. Rashi, Lev. 19:2.
2. *Sifthei Chachamim* on Rashi, Lev. 19:2.
3. Ramban, Lev. 19:2.
4. Gen. 1:27, 9:6.
5. Ramban, Lev. 19:2.
6. Exod. 20:10, 23:12, 34:21.
7. Deut. 6:18.
8. Cf. *Shevuoth* 7b.

פרשת אמור
Parashath Emor

The Cycle of Festivals

צו את בני ישראל ויקחו אליך שמן זית זך כתית למאור להעלת נר תמיד.
"COMMAND THE CHILDREN OF ISRAEL THAT THEY TAKE UNTO YOU PURE, PRESSED OLIVE OIL FOR LIGHTING, TO BRING FORTH A CONTINUOUS LIGHT." (Leviticus 24:2)

Our text repeats the commandment that the Israelites offer oil for the menorah in the sanctuary. Almost the same words are already recorded in Exodus within the description of the sanctuary and its vessels.[1] Why the repetition here?

Rashi suggests that the verse in Exodus merely foreshadows the future.[2] God tells Moshe that he will eventually direct the Israelites to offer oil. Our text is that future, when Moshe is told to command them to do just that.

Since the menorah was already lit when the sanctuary was dedicated, Ramban rejects Rashi's interpretation. Ramban therefore proposes that the original gifts of oil had been exhausted, necessitating a new appeal to replenish the reserves.[3] Yet this explanation, too, ignores the context and merely relies upon coincidence.

Or HaChayim questions both Rashi and Ramban. Its author then notes that the number seven figures prominently both in the section of the Torah dealing with the festivals, which immediately precedes our portion, and in the menorah.[4]

Netziv explains this juxtaposition by theorizing that the menorah symbolizes in-depth Torah study, an activity particularly suited to Shabbath and festivals.[5]

I would like to approach this passage with one textual introduction. Every new subject here is prefaced by the verse "God spoke to Moshe, saying."[6] However, following the section on the menorah,[7] when the Torah describes the bread to be placed upon the table in the sanctuary,[8] there is no "And God spoke to Moshe, saying." This anomaly indicates that these two subjects are one. Moreover, it suggests that the discussion of the menorah simply introduces the commandment of the *challoth*, or showbread. Rashbam suggests this relationship in his striking comments on our text,[9] and in Numbers,[10] where he explains that the menorah was to illuminate the table upon which the showbread was found. Apparently, the spiritual (the light of the menorah) is to illumine, i.e., elevate and sanctify, the material (the showbread).

If we accept this analysis, the structure of this festival section of the Torah becomes remarkable. The Torah begins enumerating the festivals with Shabbath, and concludes with the showbread, which was to be replaced each Shabbath. There seems to be a cycle here, which begins and ends with Shabbath. This configuration implies a theme of all the festivals, which reaches its crescendo on Shabbath.

Most commentaries wonder why Shabbath heads the list of festivals in our text, since Halachically the two are hardly related. After all, Shabbath is linked to Creation, the festivals to historic events; and Shabbath is a fixed day, while the *beith din* (court) determines when the festivals are celebrated. Additionally, the prohibition of work differs on Shabbath and festivals.[11]

Our thesis is very simple. All festivals commemorate significant confrontations between God and Israel within history. However, the festivals also consecrate the seasons, whose climatic changes affect the earth's productivity. Only

The Cycle of Festivals

this latter theme is emphasized in our section. Succoth alone is connected to the exodus, but — as we have already noted elsewhere — Ramban insists that this motif is not central to the festival.[12] And if this festival discussion here is based on history, where does Rosh HaShanah fit in? If, on the other hand, the underlying theme is the seasonal cycle, as expressed particularly in the agricultural productivity of the earth, then Rosh HaShanah, being the day of Creation, is part of this structure.

We must now formulate the motif stressed repeatedly in all the festivals. A nation whose economy is primarily, if not exclusively, agricultural must recognize that, despite man's genius, toil, and technical advances only God produces vegetation. The *omer* of Pesach, the two loaves of Shavuoth, and the four species of Succoth all convey the same message: The raw materials of the earth, the manufactured bread, and the amassing of grain for the winter are all the blessing of God and come to us only through His beneficence. Because this notion is so easily overlooked, due to man's immersion in agriculture, it must be reinforced constantly, especially at each season.

In discussing the main theme of Shabbath, we indicated that Rashi relates the holiness and blessing of the day to the manna, the heavenly food.[13] We also pointed out that this relationship is far from arbitrary or homiletical, for Shabbath affirms, above all, that God created the world, and natural law depends upon His will. Food generally comes from the physical or chemical interaction of heaven and earth but not always. Therefore, before enumerating the festivals — which celebrate the seasonal cycle and express thanks to God, who grants us all the bounty of the earth — the Torah records the source of this notion: Shabbath. Shabbath makes all the festivals meaningful. It heads the seasonal cycle of festivals because Shabbath's message transcends nature.

Moreover, having concluded the range of festivals, the

Torah returns to its original theme,[14] for it is so fundamental that it cannot be left merely for five festivals. Each Shabbath, the priest must enter the sanctuary and replace last week's showbread with this week's. Upon this bread, the light of the menorah shall shine, and Israel shall reiterate, "to God belong the earth and all its contents."[15]

1. Exod. 27:20.
2. Rashi, Lev. 24:2.
3. Ramban, Lev. 24:2.
4. *Or HaChayim*, Lev. 24:2.
5. *Ha'amek Davar*, Lev. 24:2.
6. See Lev. 23:1, 9, 23, 26, 33.
7. Lev. 24:1-4.
8. Ibid. 24:5.
9. Rashbam, Lev. 24:2.
10. Ibid., Num. 8:2.
11. Ramban, Lev. 23:2, discusses this problem at length.
12. Ramban, Lev. 23:36, 40.
13. See *parashath Bereishith*, "The Seventh Day."
14. Lev. 24:8.
15. Ps. 24:1.

פרשת בהר
Parashath BeHar

Commemorating Creation

את שבתתי תשמרו ומקדשי תיראו אני ה'.
"MY SHABBATHOTH YOU SHALL OBSERVE, AND MY SANCTUARY YOU SHALL REVERE — I AM THE LORD." (Leviticus 26:2)

This verse seems to conclude the preceding chapters, though they deal with social and economic laws. Additionally, it is within the Torah's discussion of holiness, particularly in the framework of the link between Shabbath and the sanctuary. Several ideas should therefore be noted at the outset.

A halachah derives from this verse's sequence of statements: The sanctuary may not be built on Shabbath.[1] Yet services in the sanctuary — sacrifices, etc., are permitted on the day of rest, although such labor is generally prohibited on Shabbath.

This relationship between the sanctuary and Shabbath reflects the structural clash of these institutions. The sanctuary is tangible; Shabbath is not. The sanctuary involves the senses; Shabbath addresses the mind and heart. The sanctuary almost borders on idolatry. This danger is countered by Shabbath, with its freedom from anything material.

What concerns us is the impact of this verse on its context. After discussing the *shemittah* (Sabbatical)[2] and *yovel* (Jubilee)[3] years, the Torah proceeds to an economic overview of Israelite society, with special emphasis upon the sale of real estate.[4] This topic leads to the sale of an individual into slavery.[5] This section culminates in a Divine pronouncement, "For the children of Israel are servants unto Me,"[6] to which the Talmud very beautifully adds, "...and not servants unto other servants."[7]

In two short phrases, our verse encapsulates this entire discussion. "My Shabbathoth" refers to the *shemittah*. This statement becomes important later, when we are warned that the Jewish community in the Holy Land will be destroyed for violating the Sabbatical year.

Furthermore, "My sanctuary" has special meaning. Elsewhere, the Torah states, "I will cut [one who engages in child sacrifices] off from among his people, for he has given of his seed to Molech in order to defile My sanctuary."[8] Ramban and Rashi's interpretation of this verse goes to the heart of our theme. They say that the "sanctuary" here is Israel itself.[9] It is an exciting notion, indeed, that Israel constitutes the sanctuary of God. Similarly, regarding defilement by contact with the dead, the Torah speaks of desecrating God's "sanctuary," a term Sforno associates with the individual Israelite.[10]

So, too, returning to our text, a Jew who sells himself into slavery has fallen deep into the abyss of defilement. The Torah therefore speaks out for the dignity, freedom, and sanctity of every Jew, who, as God's servant constitutes his sanctuary.

There is yet another dimension of our verse. It appears to conclude the Halachic matters treated in Leviticus, for what follows are simply warnings to observe the laws and descriptions of attendant rewards and punishment. Let us therefore examine it from another angle.

The Torah discusses three types of Shabbathoth. The one most familiar to us is, of course, the weekly Shabbath, commemorating creation.[11] The festivals are also called Shabbath both in the Torah[12] and in halachic literature, for we are commanded to rest on these days.[13] Interestingly, Shabbath is not called a festival, but festivals are called Shabbath. Finally, the Sabbatical and Jubilee years are certainly known as Shabbath.[14]

In a fascinating discourse, Ramban explains that these last two institutions point to the End of Days and that the fiftieth year particularly symbolizes the Messianic dream and the fulfillment of the prophetic vision of peace and harmony for all mankind. This year symbolizes the "day that is completely Shabbath."[15]

Thus, Shabbath points us in three directions. It recalls an event of the past, Creation. It commemorates the meetings between God and Israel in history, which includes the present. And it foretells a future that is beyond time — the End of Days. This multiplicity is expressed in the command "My Shabbathoth you shall observe...."

Leviticus is known as *Torath Kohanim* (the Torah of priests) ostensibly because it deals with the sanctuary, its service, and its officials, the priests. However, the laws of Leviticus also pertain to the holiness of Israel. Every area of human concern — physical, social, economic — is sanctified. The Jewish people's holiness ultimately depends upon their acceptance of God and their preaching His existence to mankind. Israel is therefore called "a kingdom of priests."[16] The term *Torath Kohanim* thus refers both to Aharon and his descendants and to the whole of Israel.

Our verse, then, sums up all of Leviticus: "My Shabbathoth you shall observe..." is directed to the kingdom of priests and its pursuit of holiness. Believing in the God who created the world, creates its history, and will create a great future of total Shabbath — this is the epitome of Israel's sanctity. "And My sanctuary you shall revere" is directed to the sons of Aharon.

Taken together in all their profundity, these two phrases constitute the essence of Leviticus.

The Depths of Simplicity

1. Rashi, Exod. 31:13.
2. Lev. 25:1-7.
3. Ibid. 25:8-13.
4. Ibid. 25:14-54.
5. Ibid. 25:35-55.
6. Ibid. 25:55.
7. *Bava Kamma* 116b.
8. Lev. 20:3.
9. Rashi and Ramban, Lev. 20:3.
10. Sforno, Num. 19:2.
11. Exod. 20:8-11.
12. Note Rashi, Lev. 23:15.
13. Note Lev. 23:7.
14. Lev. 25:2.
15. Ramban, Lev. 25:2.
16. Exod. 19:6.

פרשת בחקתי
Parashath BeChukkothai

The Uncircumcised Heart

והתודו את עונם ואת עון אבתם במעלם אשר מעלו בי....
"THEY WILL CONFESS THEIR INIQUITY AND THE INIQUITY OF THEIR FATHERS IN THEIR TRESPASS WHICH THEY TRESPASSED AGAINST ME...." (Leviticus 26:40)

After describing exile from the Land of Israel and the other tragedies to befall the Jews in their rebelliousness, the Torah begins the story of return in our text. For what is confession if not recognition of one's sins and acceptance of God's justice?

However, in the next verse, God insists, "Even I will walk with them in rebelliousness: I will bring them into the land of their enemies; perhaps then their uncircumcised heart will yield, and then they will rectify their iniquity." Surely following the people's confession, God should be more gracious and compassionate.

Noting this problem, Ibn Ezra suggests that this verse refers to God's behavior before the confession.[1] God is "taking credit" for this confession, for the Jews' exile and suffering will soften their hearts until they confess. Yet it is a strange construction.

Ramban has his own theory.[2] He sees the exhortations in Leviticus and Deuteronomy as prophecies fulfilled during the first and second exiles, respectively. By the same token, the "returns" in these two books parallel the return from Babylonian exile and the unfolding of the Messianic period. To prove his thesis, Ramban offers a fascinating and brilliant study of both texts, Deuteronomy providing especially rich support.

For our purposes, suffice it to say that, following their return from Babylonia, the Jews found enemies in their land, which was mainly under Persian dominion. Therefore, Ramban maintains, the verses follow each other. After their confession, the Jews indeed return to their land — but it remains the land of their enemies.

This passage invites several further observations:

First, the expression "perhaps then their uncircumcised heart will yield" needs explanation. Didn't the people already confess, thereby yielding?

Second, in verse 42, God promises, "I will remember My covenant with Yaakov and also My covenant with Yitzchak and also My covenant with Avraham...." The fact that the patriarchs are not mentioned chronologically has, of course, been addressed by the Midrash and the classic commentaries. Additionally, by means of the verse's cantillations, Yaakov dominates this Divine promise. Avraham and Yitzchak appear almost parenthetically.

Third, the Torah frequently attributes transgression to an "uncircumcised heart," as though something prevents the fresh, life-giving blood of faith from penetrating. Conversely, changing one's ways is very often described as removing this "covering," and allowing faith in. Yet our text predicts, "their uncircumcised heart will yield." Whereas Deuteronomy states, "The Lord, your God, will circumcise your heart."[3] What is the difference?

Two principles must be established before we can deal definitively with our text:

First, though confession is critical to repentance, the two differ greatly. Confession means recognizing one's sin and its effects. Repentance, on the other hand, implies both remorse and resolution not to repeat the crime. Only repentance atones.[4]

However there is another type of repentance — and here we lean heavily on Ramban's comments in Deuteronomy. This repentance has eschatological implications and involves man's return to his status before Adam's sin, i.e., a return to the perfection of the Garden of Eden.[5]

The chapter on repentance in Deuteronomy, as Ramban points out, describes this ultimate return to God. Here, though, we are dealing with confession and repentance vis-à-vis a particular transgression.

Our texts now take on a new dimension. Confession is followed by God's pledge to bring the people to the land of their enemies until their uncircumcised heart yields, for confession alone is only a beginning. Repentance itself is the yielding.

Second, especially according to Ramban, the sin of the Tree of Knowledge altered man's nature. For instance, we have sought physical pleasure ever since. While the Torah encourages us to transcend and sanctify the physical, there is a constant struggle between it and the spiritual. Man must always subdue his evil inclinations. Before the sin in the Garden of Eden, man was perfect, but he will not be again until the End of Days.

Therefore, in our text, the heart remains uncircumcised. Repentance weakens the impulse to sin, but that is all.

Man must continue to struggle. In contradistinction, Deuteronomy envisions ultimate repentance, through which man will reclaim the status Adam enjoyed before his transgression. Thus, repentance is called circumcision of the heart, implying the removal of sinful urges. This analysis raises many theological problems. But we rely here upon Ramban.

When one studies the three patriarchs carefully, he notes that, while Avraham and Yitzchak represent perfection, Yaakov represents reality. He errs, loses his exalted position, and dreams of sheep. He forgets to fulfill his promise. However, he rises above his failings, repents, and gains the name Yisrael. Interestingly, the Midrash relates the two goats Yaakov uses to fool his father — and thereby receive his blessing — to the two offered in atonement on Yom Kippur.[6] For Yaakov is reality. There is transgression, but it can be overcome. There is an uncircumcised heart, but it can be held in check.

Consequently, God responds to repentance by remembering His covenant with Yaakov. Avraham and Yitzchak are mentioned only indirectly.

1. Ibn Ezra, Lev. 26:41.
2. Ramban, Lev. 26:16.
3. Deut. 30:6.
4. Rambam, *Mishneh Torah*, "*Hilchoth Teshuvah*" 2:2-30.
5. Ramban, Deut. 30:6.
6. *Gen. Rabbah* 65:14.